Dagny Pullover

Easy

SIZES
S/M (L, 1X/2X).

MEASUREMENTS
Finished Bust About 48 (54, 60)"/122 (137, 152.5)cm
Finished Length About 28½ (29½, 30½)"/72.5 (75, 77.5)cm

MATERIALS
YARN
LION BRAND® Homespun® Thick & Quick®, 8oz/227g balls, each approx 160yd/146m (acrylic/polyester)
- 1 (2, 2) skein(s) in #412 Pearls (A)

LION BRAND® Wool-Ease® Thick & Quick®, 6oz/170g balls, each approx 106yd/97m (acrylic/wool)
- 5 (6, 7) balls in #099 Fisherman (B)

KNITTING NEEDLES
- One size 11 (8mm) circular needle, 40"/101.5cm long, *or size to obtain gauge*
- One size 11 (8mm) circular needle, 16"/40.5cm long

NOTIONS
- Stitch markers
- Stitch holders
- Tapestry needle

GAUGE
9 sts = about 4¼"/11cm; 14 rows = about 4½"/11.5cm in St st with A.
BE SURE TO CHECK YOUR GAUGE.

STITCH GLOSSARY
CDD (centered double decrease) Slip 2 as if to knit 2 together, knit 1, pass 2 slipped stitches over—2 sts decreased.

PATTERN STITCHES
K1, P1 RIB
(over an odd number of sts)
Row 1 K1, *p1, k1; rep from * to end of row.
Row 2 K the knit sts and p the purl sts.
Rep Row 2 for K1, p1 Rib.

Dagny Pullover

COLOR RIDGES PATTERN

Rows 1–10 With B, beg with a RS (knit) row, work in St st (k on RS, p on WS) for 10 rows.
Row 11 (RS) With A, purl.
Row 12 With A, knit.
Rep Rows 1–12 for Color Ridges pattern.

NOTES

1) Pullover is worked in 4 pieces: Back, Front, and 2 Sleeves.
2) Each piece is worked with purl ridges in Color Ridges pattern.
3) The longer circular needle is used to accommodate the sts. Work back and forth in rows on the circular needle as if working on straight needles.
4) Shorter circular needle is used for ribbed neck.
5) For smallest size only, divide yarn A into 2 separate balls before beginning.

PULLOVER
BACK

With longer circular needle and A, cast on 51 (57, 63) sts. Work in K1, p1 Rib for 3 rows.
Beg with a RS (knit) row, work in St st until piece measures about 5"/12.5cm from beg, end with a WS row as the last row you work.

First purl ridge

Next Row (RS) Purl.
Next Row Knit.

Join B.
Beg with Row 1 of pattern, work in Color Ridges pattern until piece measures about 27 (28, 29)"/68.5 (71, 73.5)cm from beg, end with a WS row as the last row you work. Cut A and continue with B only.

Shape neck and shoulders

Row 1 (RS) K19 (21, 23) sts for right shoulder, join a 2nd ball of yarn and bind off center 13 (15, 17) sts, k to end for left shoulder—19 (21, 23) sts for each shoulder.

You will now work both shoulders AT THE SAME TIME with separate balls of yarn.
Row 2 On left shoulder, bind off 9 (10, 11) sts, p to end; on right shoulder, bind off 2 sts, p to end.
Row 3 On right shoulder, bind off 9 (10, 11) sts, k to end; on left shoulder, bind off 2 sts, k to end—8 (9, 10) sts for each shoulder.
Row 4 On left shoulder, bind off rem 8 (9, 10) sts; on right shoulder, p to end.
Bind off rem 8 (9, 10) sts of right shoulder.

FRONT

Work same as Back until piece measures about 18 (19, 20)"/45.5 (48.5, 51)cm from beg, end with a WS row as the last row you work.

Shape neck

Row 1 (RS) Work in Color Ridges pattern as established over first 25 (28, 31) sts for left shoulder, join a 2nd ball of yarn and bind off center st, work in Color Ridges pattern as established to end of row for right shoulder—25 (28, 31) sts for each shoulder.
You will now work both shoulders AT THE SAME TIME with separate balls of yarn.
Row 2 Work in Color Ridges pattern across both shoulders, using separate balls of yarn.
Row 3 On left shoulder, work Color Ridges pattern to last 3 sts, k2tog, k1; on right shoulder, k1, ssk, work in Color Ridges pattern to end—24 (27, 30) sts for each shoulder.
Rows 4–6 Work even in Color Ridges pattern over both shoulders, using separate balls of yarn, for 3 rows.
Row 7 Rep Row 3—23 (26, 29) sts for each shoulder.
Rows 8–13 Rep Rows 2–7 once more—21 (24, 27) sts for each shoulder.

Work even in Color Ridges pattern as established over both shoulders, using separate balls of yarn, until piece measures about 25 (25½, 26)"/63.5 (65, 66)cm, end with a WS row as the last row you work.

Next Row (RS) On left shoulder, work in Color Ridges pattern to last 3 sts, k2tog, k1; on right shoulder, k1, ssk, work in Color Ridges pattern to end—20 (23, 26) sts for each shoulder.

Dagny Pullover

Next Row Work even in Color Ridges pattern over both shoulders, using separate balls of yarn.
Rep last 2 rows 2 (3, 4) more times—18 (20, 22) sts. Cut A.

Shape shoulders and continue shaping neck

Work with B only to end of piece.
Row 1 (RS) On left shoulder, bind off 9 (10, 11) sts, k to last 3 sts, k2tog, k1; on right shoulder, k1, ssk, k to end.
Row 2 On right shoulder, bind off 9 (10, 11) sts, p to end; on left shoulder, p to end—8 (9, 10) sts for each shoulder.
Row 3 On left shoulder, bind off rem 8 (9, 10) sts; on right shoulder, k to end.
Bind off rem 8 (9, 10) sts of right shoulder.

SLEEVES (MAKE 2)

With longer circular needle and A, cast on 27 (29, 31) sts. Work in K1, p1 Rib for 3 rows.

Beg with a RS (knit) row, work in St st until piece measures about 5"/12.5cm from beg, end with a WS (purl) row as the last row you work.

First purl ridge

Next Row (RS) Purl.
Next Row Knit.
Change to B.

SIZE S/M ONLY

Rows 1–9 Work Rows 1–9 of Color Ridges pattern.
Inc Row 10 With B, p1, M1P, p to last st, M1P, P1—29 sts.
Row 11 With A, purl.
Row 12 With A, knit.
Rep Rows 1–12—31 sts.
Work even in Color Ridges pattern as established until piece measures about 17"/43cm from beg, end with a WS row as the last row you work.

SIZE L ONLY

Rows 1–3 Work Rows 1–3 of Color Ridges pattern.
Inc Row 4 With B, p1, M1P, p to last st, M1P, P1—31 sts.
Rows 5–9 Work Rows 5–9 of Color Ridges pattern.
Row 10 Rep Row 4—33 sts.
Row 11 With A, purl.
Row 12 With A, knit.
Rep Rows 1–4—35 sts.
Work even in Color Ridges pattern as established until piece measures about 16½"/42cm from beg, end with a WS row as the last row you work.

SIZE 1X/2X ONLY

Row 1 Work Row 1 of Color Ridges pattern.
Inc Row 2 With B, p1, M1P, p to last st, M1P, P1—33 sts.
Rows 3–5 Work Rows 3–5 of Color Ridges pattern.
Row 6 Rep Row 2—35 sts.
Rows 7–9 Work Rows 7–9 of Color Ridges pattern.
Row 10 Rep Row 2—37 sts.
Row 11 With A, purl.

Row 12 With A, knit.
Rep Rows 1 and 2—39 sts.
Work even in Color Ridges pattern as established until piece measures about 16"/40.5cm from beg, end with a WS row as the last row you work.

Shape Cap

Work with B only to end of piece.
Row 1 (RS) Bind off 5 (6, 7) sts, k to end of row—26 (29, 32) sts.
Row 2 Bind off 5 (6, 7) sts, p to end of row—21 (23, 25) sts.
Rows 3 and 4 Rep Rows 1 and 2—11 sts.
Bind off rem 11 sts.

FINISHING

Sew shoulder seams.

Ribbed neck

From RS, with shorter needle and B, beg at left shoulder seam, pick up and k 18 sts evenly spaced along left front neck edge, 1 st at center front neck, 18 sts along right front neck edge, and 19 (21, 23) sts across back neck—56 (58, 60) sts.
Place marker and join by working the first st on the left needle with the working yarn from the right needle.
Rnd 1 K1, *p1, k1; rep from * to 1 st before center front st, CDD, pm on st just made, **k1, p1; rep from ** to end of rnd.
Rnds 2–6 K the knit sts and p the purl sts to 1 st before marked st, CDD, pm on st just made, k the knits sts and p the purl sts to end of rnd.
Bind off in rib.

Place markers on side edges of Back and Front, about 7 (8, 9)"/18 (20.5, 23)cm below shoulder seams. Sew tops of Sleeves between markers.
Sew side and Sleeve seams.

Weave in ends. •

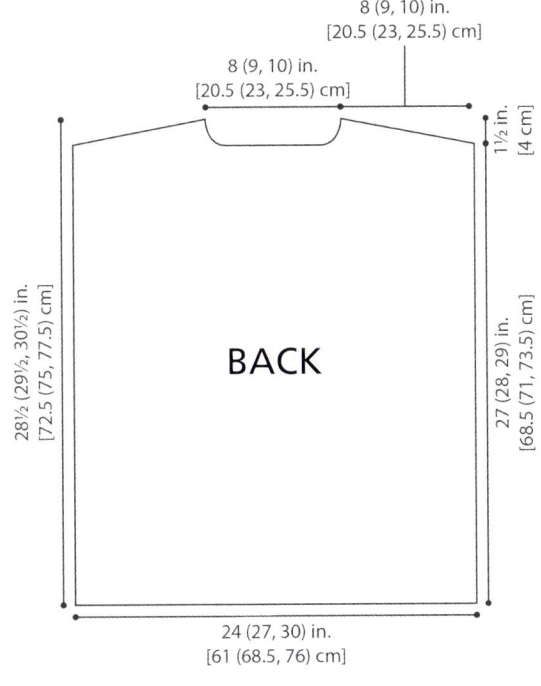

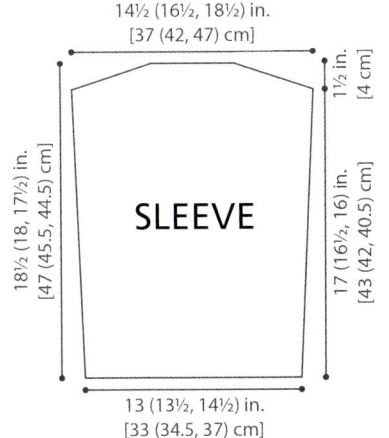

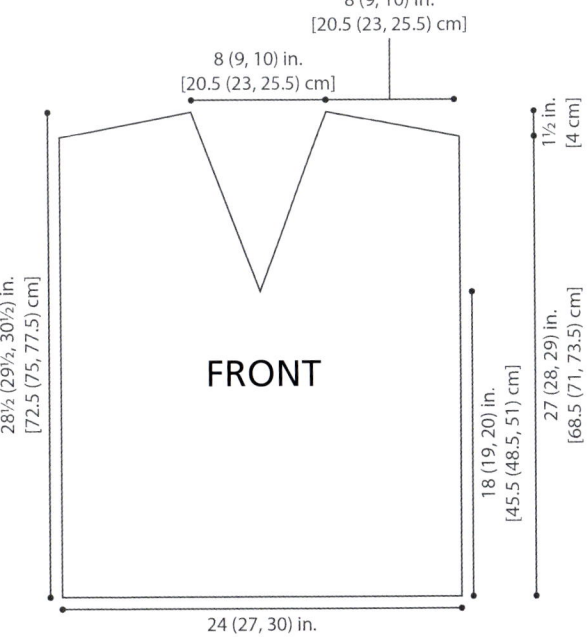

Marble Hill Pullover

Easy

SIZES
XS (S, M, L, 1X, 2X, 3X).

MEASUREMENTS
Finished Chest About 34 (38, 42, 46, 50, 54, 58)"/86.5 (96.5, 106.5, 117, 127, 137, 147.5)cm
Finished Length About 22½ (23½, 24½, 25, 26, 26½, 27)"/57 (59.5, 62, 63.5, 66, 67.5, 68.5)cm

MATERIALS
YARN
LION BRAND® Mandala®, 5.3oz/150g balls, each approx 590yd/540m (acrylic)
- 2 (2, 3, 3, 3, 4, 4) balls in #212 Spirit

KNITTING NEEDLES
- One pair size 8 (5mm) needles, *or size to obtain gauge*
- One pair size 6 (4mm) needles

NOTIONS
- Tapestry needle

GAUGE
20½ sts + 29½ rows = about 4"/10cm in St st with larger needles. *BE SURE TO CHECK YOUR GAUGE.*

PATTERN STITCH
K2, P2 RIB
(multiple of 4 sts + 2 additional sts)
Row 1 (WS) K2, *p2, k2; rep from * to end of row.
Row 2 K the knit sts and p the purl sts.
Rep Row 2 for K2, p2 Rib.

NOTES
1) Pullover is made in 4 pieces: Back, Front, and 2 Sleeves.
2) All pieces are worked in St st, with ribbed lower edges.

PULLOVER
BACK
With smaller needles, cast on 86 (94, 106, 114, 126, 134, 146) sts.
Work in K2, p2 Rib until piece measures about 1½"/4cm from beg, end with a WS row as the last row you work. Change to larger needles.

SIZES XS (M, 1X, 3X) ONLY
Inc Row (RS) Kfb, k to end of row—you will now have 87 (107, 127, 147) sts.

SIZES S (L, 2X) ONLY
Inc Row (RS) Kfb, k46 (56, 66), kfb, k to last st, kfb—you will now have 97 (117, 137) sts.

Beg with a WS (purl) row, work in St st (k on RS, p on WS) until piece measures about 15"/38cm from beg, end with a WS (purl) row as the last row you work.

Shape raglan armholes
Next Row Bind off 6 (6, 7, 7, 7, 8, 8) sts, k to end of row.
Next Row Bind off 6 (6, 7, 7, 7, 8, 8) sts, p to end of row—you will now have 75 (85, 93, 103, 113, 121, 131) sts.

Dec Row 1 (RS) K1, k2tog, k to last 3 sts, k2tog tbl, k1—73 (83, 91, 101, 111, 119, 129) sts.
Row 2 Purl.
Rep Rows 1 and 2 for 1 (7, 8, 14, 20, 25, 33) more times—71 (69, 75, 73, 71, 69, 63) sts.
Work even in St st for 2 rows.

Marble Hill Pullover

Rep Row 1—69 (67, 73, 71, 69, 67, 61) sts.
Work even in St st for 3 rows.
Rep last 4 rows 11 (10, 11, 9, 8, 6, 3) more times—47 (47, 51, 53, 53, 55, 55) sts.
Bind off.

FRONT

Cast on and work same as Back to Shape Raglan Armholes.

Shape Raglan Armholes

Next Row Bind off 6 (6, 7, 7, 7, 8, 8) sts, k to end of row.
Next Row Bind off 6 (6, 7, 7, 7, 8, 8) sts, p to end of row—you will now have 75 (85, 93, 103, 113, 121, 131) sts.
Dec Row 1 (RS) K1, k2tog, k to last 3 sts, k2tog tbl, k1—73 (83, 91, 101, 111, 119, 129) sts.
Row 2 Purl.
Rep Rows 1 and 2 for 1 (7, 8, 14, 20, 25, 33) more times—71 (69, 75, 73, 71, 69, 63) sts.
Work even in St st for 2 rows.

Rep Row 1—69 (67, 73, 71, 69, 67, 61) sts.
Work even in St st for 3 rows.
Rep last 4 rows 9 (8, 9, 7, 6, 4, 1) more time(s)—51 (51, 55, 57, 57, 59, 59) sts.

Shape Neck

Row 1 (RS) K9 for left side of neck, join a 2nd ball of yarn and bind off next 33 (33, 37, 39, 39, 41, 41) sts, k to end of row for right side of neck—9 sts on each side of neck. You will now be working both sides of the neck AT THE SAME TIME using separate balls of yarn.
Row 2 On first side, work in St st to end of side; on 2nd side, bind off 3 sts, work in St st to end of side—6 sts on left side of neck and 9 sts on right side of neck.
Row 3 On first side, k1, k2tog, work in St st to end of side; on 2nd side, bind off 3 sts, work in St st to last 3 sts, k2tog tbl, k1—5 sts on each side of neck.

Rows 4 and 5 On first side, work in St st to end of side; on 2nd side, bind off 2 sts, work in St st to end of side—3 sts on each side.
Row 6 Purl across sts on both sides.
Row 7 On first side, k1, k2tog; on 2nd side, k2tog tbl, k1. Bind off rem 2 sts on each side.

SLEEVES (MAKE 2)

With smaller needles, cast on 42 (42, 46, 46, 46, 50, 50) sts.
Work in K2, p2 Rib until piece measures about 1¼"/3cm from beg, end with a WS row as the last row you work.

Change to larger needles.
Beg with a RS (knit) row, work in St st for 2 rows.
Inc Row (RS) K3, kfb, k to last 5 sts, kfb, k4—44 (44, 48, 48, 48, 52, 52) sts.
Work even in St st for 3 rows.
Rep last 4 rows 0 (2, 0, 0, 4, 1, 12) more times—44 (48, 48, 48, 56, 54, 76) sts.

Rep Inc Row—46 (50, 50, 50, 58, 56, 78) sts.
Work even in St st for 5 rows.
Rep last 6 rows 15 (14, 15, 16, 14, 16, 9) more times—76 (78, 80, 82, 86, 88, 96) sts when all inc have been completed.

Continue even in St st until piece measures about 17 (17, 17, 18, 18, 18, 18½)"/43 (43, 43, 45.5, 45.5, 45.5, 47)cm from beg, end with a WS row as the last row you work.

Shape raglans

Next Row Bind off 6 (6, 7, 7, 7, 8, 8) sts, k to end of row.
Next Row Bind off 6 (6, 7, 7, 7, 8, 8) sts, p to end of row—64 (66, 66, 68, 72, 72, 80) sts.
Dec Row 1 (RS) K1, k2tog, work in St st to last 3 sts, k2tog tbl, k1—62 (64, 64, 66, 70, 70, 78) sts.
Row 2 Purl.

Rep Rows 1 and 2 for 19 (17, 14, 10, 10, 9, 15) more times—24 (30, 36, 46, 50, 52, 48) sts when all dec have been completed.
Work even in St st for 2 rows.

Rep Row 1—22 (28, 34, 44, 48, 50, 46) sts.
Work even in St st for 3 rows.
Rep last 4 rows 2 (5, 8, 11, 13, 14, 12) more times—18 (18, 18, 22, 22, 22, 22) sts.
Bind off.

FINISHING

Sew Sleeves to Front and Back along raglans, leaving one raglan seam unsewn.

Neckband

From RS with smaller needles, beg at unsewn raglan, pick up and k 106 (106, 110, 114, 122, 126, 126) sts evenly spaced along Front and Back necks and tops of Sleeves.
Work in K2, p2 Rib for about ¾"/2cm.
Bind off loosely in rib.

Sew remaining raglan seam including neckband.
Sew side and Sleeve seams.

Weave in ends. •

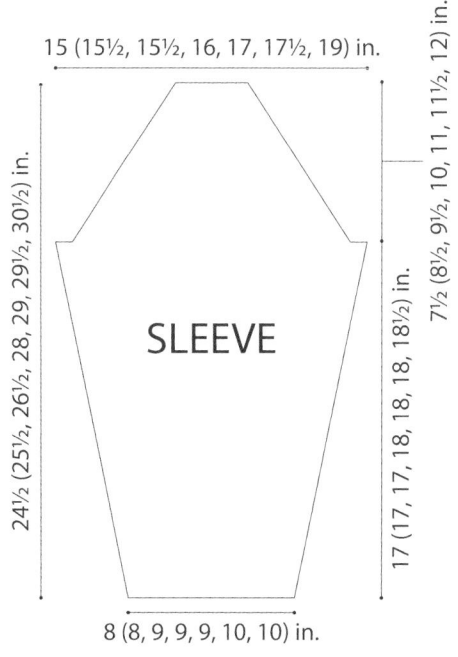

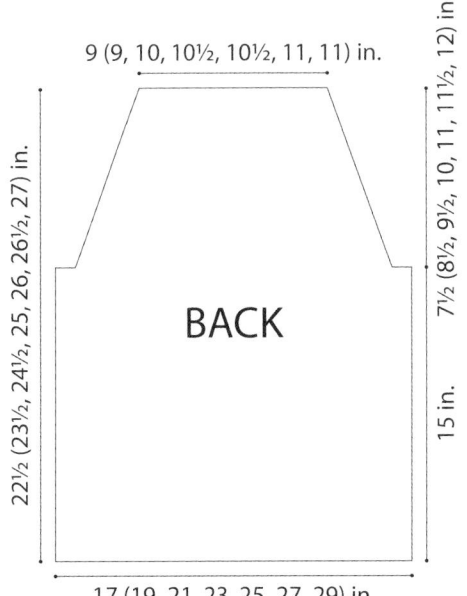

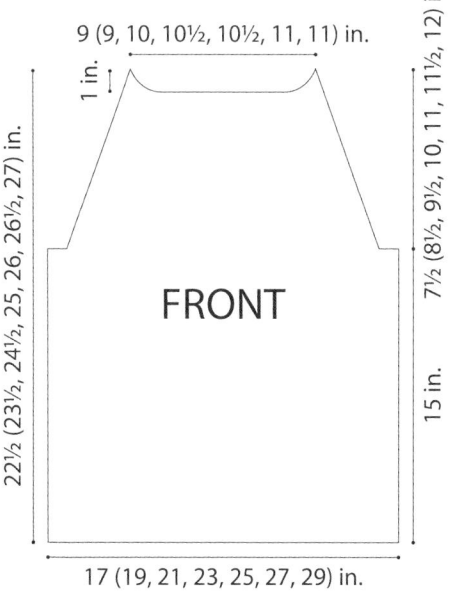

Cropped Drop Stitch Pullover

Intermediate

SIZES
XS/S (M/L, 1X/2X).

MEASUREMENTS
Finished Bust 39 (46, 54)"/99 (117, 137)cm
Finished Length 16½ (18, 19½)"/42 (45.5, 49.5)cm
Finished Waist 31 (38, 46)"/78.5 (96.5, 117)cm

MATERIALS
YARN
LION BRAND® Hometown®, 5oz/142g balls, each approx 81yd/74m (acrylic)
- 5 (7, 9) balls in #101 Providence Pink

KNITTING NEEDLES
- One size 11 (8mm) circular needle, 29"/73.5cm long, *or size to obtain gauge*

NOTIONS
- Stitch markers
- Stitch holders
- Tapestry needle

GAUGE
10 sts + 14 rows = about 4"/10cm in St st.
BE SURE TO CHECK YOUR GAUGE.

NOTES
1) Pullover is worked sideways in one piece from the left sleeve across to right sleeve.
2) A circular needle is used to accommodate the number of stitches. Work back and forth in rows on the circular needle as if working on straight needles.
3) When binding off, sts are dropped to create a "ladder" effect.
4) Piece is folded in half and seamed following a diagram.

PULLOVER
LEFT SLEEVE
Cast on 25 sts.
Work in St st (k on RS, p on WS) until piece measures about 12½ (11, 10)"/32 (28, 25.5)cm from beg, end with a WS row as the last row you work.

Shape left sleeve
Inc Row 1 (RS) K2, M1, k to last 2 sts, M1, k2—you will have 27 sts in this row.
Row 2 Purl.
Rep last 2 rows 9 (11, 13) more times—you will have 45 (49, 53) sts after all inc have been made.

SHAPE BODY
Row 1 (RS) Cast on 4 (4, 5) sts, k to end of row—49 (53, 58) sts.
Row 2 Cast on 4 (4, 5) sts, p to end of row—53 (57, 63) sts.
Rows 3 and 4 Rep Rows 1 and 2—61 (65, 73) sts in Row 4.
Row 5 Cast on 4 (5, 5) sts, k to end of row—65 (70, 78) sts.
Row 6 Cast on 4 (5, 5) sts, p to end of row—69 (75, 83) sts.
Row 7 Rep Row 5—73 (80, 88) sts.
Row 8 Cast on 4 (5, 5) sts, beg with sts just cast-on, k4 sts, p to last 4 sts, k4—77 (85, 93) sts.
Row 9 Knit.
Row 10 K4, p to last 4 sts, k4.
Rep the last 2 rows 1 (4, 7) more times.

Cropped Drop Stitch Pullover

Inc Row (RS) K37 (41, 45), M1, [k1, M1] twice, k to end of row—80 (88, 96) sts.

Divide for neck

Next Row (WS) K4, p33 (37, 41), k3, place rem 40 (44, 48) sts onto a holder for back—40 (44, 48) sts rem on needle for Front.

FRONT

Row 1 (RS) Knit.
Row 2 K4, p to last 3 sts, k3.
Rep Rows 1 and 2 for 20 more times.
Place these 40 (44, 48) front sts onto a separate holder and cut yarn.

BACK

Place 40 (44, 48) back sts from holder onto needle, and join yarn so that you are ready to work a WS row.
Row 1 (WS) K3, p to last 4 sts, k4.
Row 2 Knit.
Rep Rows 1 and 2 for 20 more times.
Rep Row 1 once more.

Rejoin work

Next Row (RS) K across 40 (44, 48) back sts, then k across 40 (44, 48) sts from front holder—you will have 80 (88, 96) sts at the end of this row.
Dec Row K4, p33 (37, 41), [p2tog] 3 times, p to last 4 sts, k4—77 (85, 93) sts.
Next Row Knit.
Next Row K4, p to last 4 sts, k4.
Rep last 2 rows 1 (4, 7) more times.

SHAPE BODY

Row 1 (RS) Bind off 4 (5, 5) sts, k to end of row—73 (80, 88) sts.
Row 2 Bind off 4 (5, 5) sts, p to end of row—69 (75, 83) sts.
Rows 3 and 4 Rep Rows 1 and 2—61 (65, 73) sts in Row 4.
Row 5 Bind off 4 (4, 5) sts, k to end of row—57 (61, 68) sts.
Row 6 Bind off 4 (4, 5) sts, p to end of row—53 (57, 63) sts.
Rows 7 and 8 Rep Rows 5 and 6—45 (49, 53) sts in Row 8.
Place markers at each end of last row.

Shape right sleeve

Dec Row 1 (RS) K1, ssk, k to last 3 sts, k2tog, k1—43 (47, 51) sts.
Row 2 Purl.
Rep last 2 rows 9 (11, 13) more times—25 sts rem.

Work in St st until piece measures about 18"/45.5cm from marked row, end with a WS row as the last row you work. Bind off as follows:

Bind off 9 sts, *drop next st from left hand needle and allow to unravel all the way down to cast-on edge (to make a "ladder"), stretch the st on the right hand needle to about 1"/2.5cm, bind off 3 sts; rep from * once more, bind off to end of row.

FINISHING

Following diagram, fold piece in half. Matching Edge 1 to Edge 2 and Edge 3 to Edge 4, sew side and sleeve seams.

Weave in ends. •

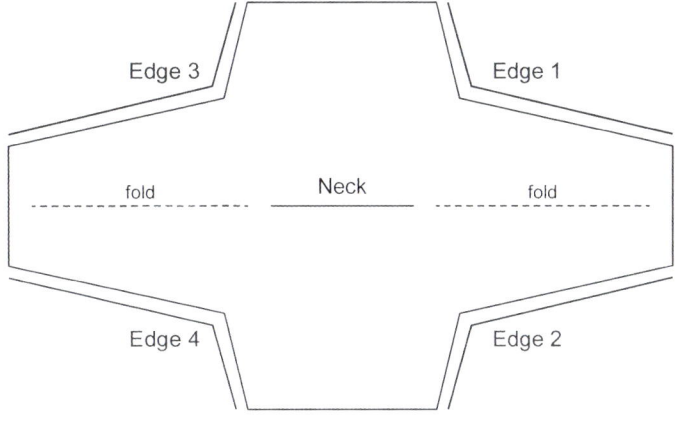

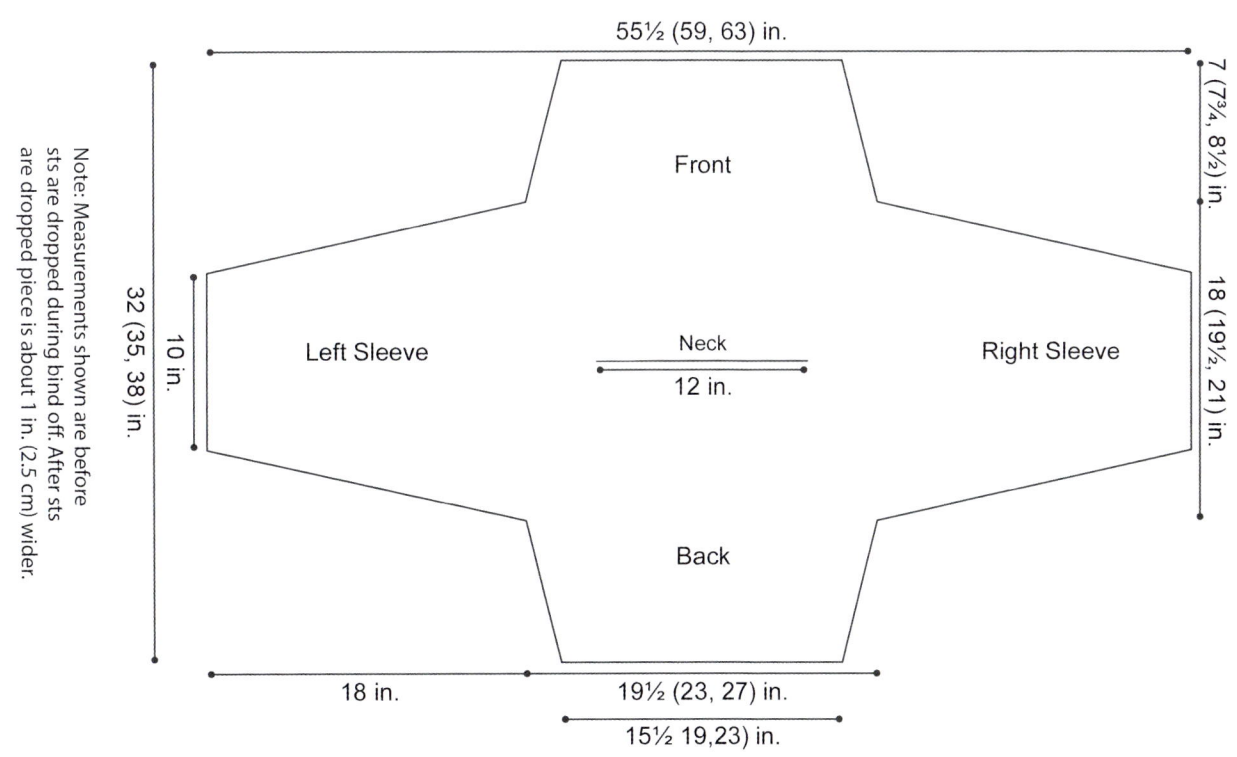

Cozy Collared Pullover

Easy

SIZES
XS/S (L).

MEASUREMENTS
Finished Bust About 52 (62)"/132 (157.5)
Finished Length About 23½ (24½)"/59.5 (62)cm

MATERIALS
YARN
LION BRAND® Wool-Ease® Thick & Quick®, 6oz/170g balls, each approx 106yd/97m (acrylic/wool)
- 5 (7) balls in #099 Fisherman (A)

LION BRAND® Homespun® Thick & Quick®, 8oz/227g balls, each approx 160yd/146m (acrylic/polyester)
- 2 (3) balls in #412 Pearls (B)

KNITTING NEEDLES
- One size 15 (10mm) circular needle, 36"/91.5cm long, *or size to obtain gauge*
- One size 13 (9mm) circular needle, 16"/40.5cm long
- One size 13 (9mm) circular needle, 24"/61cm long
- One size 13 (9mm) circular needle, 36"/91.5cm long

NOTIONS
- Stitch markers
- Tapestry needle

GAUGE
8 sts + 16 rows = about 4"/10cm in Ridge st with larger needle with A and B.
BE SURE TO CHECK YOUR GAUGE.

PATTERN STITCHES
K2, P2 RIB
(over a multiple of 4 sts + 2 additional sts)
Row 1 (WS) K2, *p2, k2; rep from * to end of row.
Row 2 K the knit sts and p the purl sts.
Rep Row 2 for K2, p2 Rib.

RIDGE STITCH
Row 1 (RS) With B, knit.
Row 2 With B, purl.
Rows 3 and 4 With A, knit.
Rep Rows 1–4 for Ridge st.

NOTES
1) Pullover is worked in 4 pieces: Front, Back, and 2 Sleeves.
2) A circular needle is used to accommodate the large number of sts. Work back and forth on the circular needle as if working on straight needles.
3) Collar is worked in the round on circular needle from sts picked up around neck edge.

PULLOVER
BACK
With longest 13 (9mm) needle and A, cast on 62 (74) sts. Beg with a Row 1, work in K2, p2 Rib until piece measures about 7"/18cm from beg, end with a RS row as the last row you work.
Dec Row (WS) [K2, p2tog, k2, p2, k2tog, p2] 5 (6) times, k2—you will have 52 (62) sts at the end of this row. Change to largest circular needle and B, and beg with Row 1, work in Ridge st until piece measures about 22 (23)"/56 (58.5)cm from beg, end with a WS row as the last row you work.

Cozy Collared Pullover

Shape shoulders
Continuing in Ridge st, bind off 2 (4) sts at beg of next 2 rows, 3 (4) sts at beg of next 6 rows, then 4 sts at beg of next 4 rows.
Bind off rem 14 sts for back neck.

FRONT
Cast on and work same as for Back until piece measures about 20½ (21½)"/52 (54.5)cm from beg, end with a WS row as the last row you work.

Shape neck
Mark center 4 sts.
Next Row (RS) Continuing in Ridge st, work to marked sts, join a 2nd ball of yarn and bind off marked center 4 sts, work to end of row—24 (29) sts rem on each side.
You will now be working both sides AT THE SAME TIME using separate balls of yarn.
Next 2 Rows Continuing in Ridge st, on first side, work to end of side; on 2nd side, bind off 2 sts, work to end of side.
Next 6 Rows Continuing in Ridge st, on first side, work to end of side; on 2nd side, bind off 1 st, work to end of side—19 (24) sts on each side when all bind offs have been completed.
Continuing in Ridge st, work both sides AT THE SAME TIME with separate balls of yarn until piece measures same as Back to shoulders.

Shape shoulders
Continue in Ridge st as you work the following rows.
Next 2 Rows On first side, bind off 2 (4) sts, work to end of side; on 2nd side, work to end of side—17 (20) sts on each side.
Next 6 Rows On first side, bind off 3 (4) sts, work to end of side; on 2nd side, work to end of side—8 sts on each side.
Next 2 Rows On first side, bind off 4 sts, work to end of side; on 2nd side, work to end of side—4 sts on each side.

Next Row On first side, bind off rem 4 sts; on 2nd side, work to end of row.
Bind off rem 4 sts.

SLEEVES (MAKE 2)

With largest circular needle and B, cast on 26 (28) sts.
Knit 10 rows.
Change to A and beg with a RS (knit) row, work in St st (k on RS, p on WS) for 4 rows.
Inc Row (RS) K1, kfb, k to last 2 sts, kfb, k1—you will have 28 (30) sts at the end of this row.
Continue in St st for 5 rows.
Rep last 6 rows 3 (4) more times—34 (38) sts when all inc have been completed.
Continue in St st until piece measures about 13"/33cm from beg, end with a WS row as the last row you work.
Change to B and knit 10 rows.
Bind off.

FINISHING

Sew Back to Front at shoulders. Place markers on Front and Back 8 (9)"/20.5 (23)cm down from shoulder seams. Sew Sleeves between markers. Sew side and Sleeve seams.

Collar

From RS with shortest size 13 (9mm) needle and A, and beginning at one shoulder seam, pick up and k 34 sts evenly spaced around neck edge. Place marker for beg of rnd. Join by working the first st on the left hand needle with the working yarn from the right hand needle.
Rnd 1 (RS) *K1, p1; rep from * around.
Rep Rnd 1 for 5 more rnds.
Change to medium length size 13 (9mm) circular needle as you work the next rnd.
Inc Rnd *Kfb, pfb; rep from * around—68 sts.
Next Rnd *K2, p2; rep from * around.
Rep last rnd until collar measures about 14"/35.5cm.
Bind off in k2, p2 pattern.

Weave in ends. •

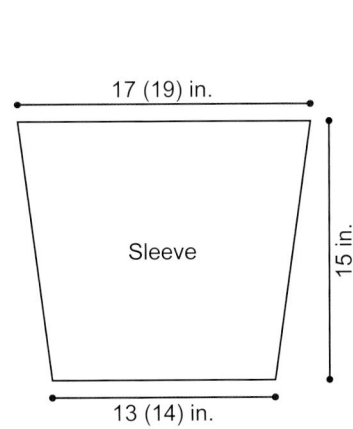

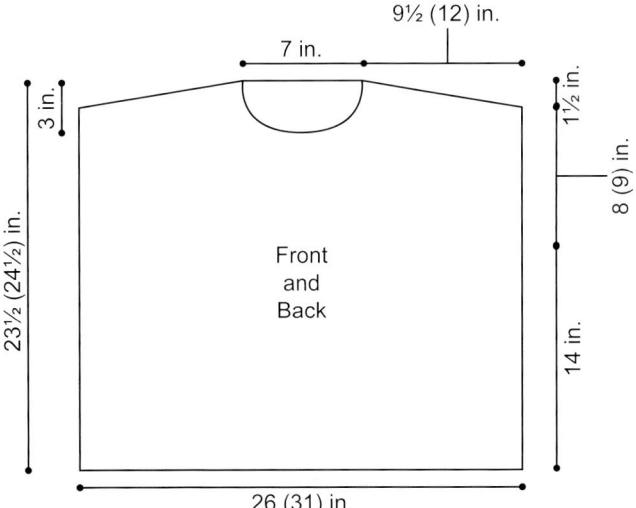

Mother and Child Pullovers

Easy

SIZES
Child 2 (Child 4, Child 6) (Women's S, Women's M, Women's L).

MEASUREMENTS
Finished Bust About 28½ (32, 35½) (41, 44½, 48)"/72.5 (81.5, 90) (104, 113, 122)cm
Finished Length About 16½ (17½, 18½) (21, 22, 23)"/42 (44.5, 47) (53.5, 56, 58.5)cm

MATERIALS
YARN
LION BRAND® Pound of Love®, 16oz/454g balls, each approx 1,020yd/932m (acrylic)
- 1 ball each in #134 Terracotta (A), #178 Maize (B), #100 White (C), #121 Barley (D), and #126 Umber (E)

KNITTING NEEDLES
- One size 8 (5mm) circular needle, 24"/61cm long for child sizes, 36"/91.5cm long for adult sizes, *or size to obtain gauge*
- One size 8 (5mm) circular needle, 16"/40.5cm long

NOTIONS
- Stitch markers and holders
- Tapestry needle

GAUGE
18 sts + 21 rows/rnds = about 4"/10cm in Charted Fair Isle pattern.
BE SURE TO CHECK YOUR GAUGE.

PATTERN STITCHES
K1, P1 RIB WORKED IN ROWS
(over an even number of sts)
Row 1 *K1, p1; rep from * to end of row.
Row 2 K the knit sts and p the purl sts.
Rep Row 2 for K1, p1 Rib worked in rows.

K1, P1 RIB WORKED IN RNDS
(over an even number of sts)
Rnd 1 *K1, p1; rep from * to end of rnd.
Rnd 2 K the knit sts and p the purl sts.
Rep Rnd 2 for K1, p1 Rib worked in rnds.

NOTES
1) Yarn amount listed, one ball of each color, is sufficient to make one adult size (S–L) AND one child size (2–6).
2) Pullover is made in 3 pieces; Body and 2 Sleeves.
3) Body is worked in rnds from lower edge up underarms. Piece is then divided and Front and Back are worked back and forth in rows to shoulders. Sleeves are worked separately, back and forth in rows.
4) All pieces begin with a ribbed lower edge. Remainder of each piece is worked in St st, changing color following a Fair Isle pattern Chart.
5) Stitches are picked up around neck edge for neckband.

CHART NOTES
1) There are 2 Charts, 1 for child sizes and 1 for adult sizes.
2) The Fair Isle patterns are worked following Charts. When working in rnds, read all rnds of Chart from right to left. When working in rows, read RS rows of Chart from right to left and WS rows from left to right.
3) When changing yarn color, do not cut old color. Carry color not in use across WS of piece.
4) When you've worked last rnd/row shown on Chart, begin again with rnd/row 1.

PULLOVER
BODY

With longer needle and A, cast on 128 (144, 160) (184, 200, 216) sts.

Place marker for beg of rnd. Join by working first st on left-hand needle with working yarn from right-hand needle and being careful not to twist sts.

Work in K1, p1 rib worked in rnds until piece measures about 1½ (1½, 1½) (2½, 2½, 2½)"/4 (4, 4) (6.5, 6.5, 6.5)cm from beg.

Knit 1 rnd. Cut A.

Begin charted Fair Isle pattern

Note Use Chart that matches your sweater size!
Work in St st worked in rnds (k every st of every rnd) and change yarn color following Fair Isle Chart until Body measures about 10 (10½, 11) (13, 13½, 14)"/25.5 (26.5, 28) (33, 34.5, 35.5)cm from beg.

Divide for armholes

Next Row (RS) Work as established over first 64 (72, 80) (92, 100, 108) sts, place rem sts on a holder for front —you will have 64 (72, 80) (92, 100, 108) sts rem on needle for back and 64 (72, 80) (92, 100, 108) sts on a holder for front.

BACK

Working back and forth in rows over back sts only, work in St st worked in rows (k on RS, p on WS) and continue to change color following Fair Isle Chart until back measures about 5½ (6, 6½) (7, 7½, 8)"/14 (15, 16.5) (18, 19, 20.5)cm from divide, end with a WS row.

Mother and Child Pullovers

Place marker on each side of center 22 (24, 26) (32, 34, 36) sts for back neck.

Shape right back neck and shoulder

Next Row (RS) Bind off 6 (7, 8) (9, 10, 11) sts, work as established to first back neck marker, place 22 (24, 26) (32, 34, 36) neck sts between markers on a holder, place rem 21 (24, 27) (30, 33, 36) sts on another holder for left shoulder—15 (17, 19) (21, 23, 25) sts rem on needle for right shoulder.

Next Row Bind off 2 sts, work as established to end of row—13 (15, 17) (19, 21, 23) sts.

Next Row Bind off 6 (7, 8) (9, 10, 11) sts, work as established to end of row—7 (8, 9) (10, 11, 12) sts.

Next Row P2tog, work as established to end of row—6 (7, 8) (9, 10, 11) sts.

Bind off.

Shape left back neck and shoulder

Return 21 (24, 27) (30, 33, 36) left shoulder sts to needle, ready to work a RS row. Join yarn.

Next Row (RS) Bind off 2 sts, work as established to end of row—19 (22, 25) (28, 31, 34) sts.

Next Row Bind off 6 (7, 8) (9, 10, 11) sts, work as established to end of row—13 (15, 17) (19, 21, 23) sts.

Next Row K2tog, work as established to end of row—12 (14, 16) (18, 20, 22) sts.

Next Row Bind off 6 (7, 8) (9, 10, 11) sts, work as established to end of row—6 (7, 8) (9, 10, 11) sts.

Next Row Work as established to end of row.

Bind off.

FRONT

Return 64 (72, 80) (92, 100, 108) front sts to needle, ready to work a RS row.

Work same as for Back until front measures about 2½ (3, 3½) (4, 4½, 5)"/6.5 (7.5, 9) (10, 11.5, 12.5)cm from divide, end with a WS row.

Place marker on each side of center 12 (14, 16) (22, 24, 26) sts for front neck.

Shape left front neck and shoulder

Row 1 (RS) Work as established to first front neck marker, place 12 (14, 16) (22, 24, 26) sts between markers on a holder for neck, place rem 26 (29, 32) (35, 38, 41) sts on another holder for right shoulder—26 (29, 32) (35, 38, 41) sts rem on needle for left shoulder.

Row 2 Bind off 3 sts, work as established to end of row—23 (26, 29) (32, 35, 38) sts.

Row 3 Work as established to end of row.

Row 4 Bind off 2 sts, work as established to end of row—21 (24, 27) (30, 33, 36) sts.

Row 5 Work as established to end of row.

Row 6 Bind off 1 st, work as established to end of row—20 (23, 26) (29, 32, 35) sts.

Rows 7–10 Rep Rows 5 and 6 twice more—18 (21, 24) (27, 30, 33) sts rem in Row 10.

Work even as established until left front measures same as left back to beg of back shoulder shaping, end with a WS row.

Next Row (RS) Bind off 6 (7, 8) (9, 10, 11) sts, work as established to end of row—12 (14, 16) (18, 20, 22) sts.

Next Row Work even as established to end of row.

Next 2 Rows Rep last 2 rows—6 (7, 8) (9, 10, 11) sts.

Bind off.

Shape right front neck and shoulder

Return 26 (29, 32) (35, 38, 41) right shoulder sts to needle, ready to work a RS row. Join yarn.

Row 1 (RS) Bind off 3 sts, work as established to end of row—23 (26, 29) (32, 35, 38) sts.

Row 2 Work as established to end of row.

Row 3 Bind off 2 sts, work as established to end of row—21 (24, 27) (30, 33, 36) sts.

Row 4 Work as established to end of row.

Row 5 Bind off 1 st, work as established to end of row—20 (23, 26) (29, 32, 35) sts.

Rows 6–9 Rep last 2 rows twice more—18 (21, 24) (27, 30, 33) sts in Row 9.

Work even as established until right front measures same as right back to beg of back shoulder shaping, end with a RS row.

Next Row (WS) Bind off 6 (7, 8) (9, 10, 11) sts, work as established to end of row—12 (14, 16) (18, 20, 22) sts.

Next Row Work even as established to end of row.
Next 2 Rows Rep last 2 rows—6 (7, 8) (9, 10, 11) sts.
Bind off.

SLEEVES (MAKE 2)

With shorter needle and A, cast on 32 (36, 40) (44, 48, 52) sts.
Work in K1, p1 Rib worked in rows until piece measures about 1½ (1½, 1½) (2½, 2½, 2½)"/4 (4, 4) (6.5, 6.5, 6.5)cm from beg, end with a WS row.

Begin charted Fair Isle pattern

Work remainder of Sleeve in St st worked in rows (k on RS, p on WS) and change yarn color following Fair Isle Chart.
Inc Row (RS) Work in pattern over first st, M1, work as established to last st, M1, work last st—34 (38, 42) (46, 50, 54) sts.

Work even as established, changing yarn color following Fair Isle Chart for 5 (5, 5) (7, 7, 7) rows.
Rep Inc Row—36 (40, 44) (48, 52, 56) sts.
Rep these 6 (6, 6) (8, 8, 8) rows for 7 (7, 7) (8, 8, 8) more times, working added sts into Fair Isle pattern—50 (54, 58) (64, 68, 72) sts when all inc have been completed.

Work even as established until piece measures about 11 (11, 11) (18, 18, 18)"/28 (28, 28) (45.5, 45.5, 45.5)cm from beg, end with a WS row.

Shape sleeve cap

Continuing in pattern, bind off 5 (5, 5) (3, 3, 3) sts at beg of next 8 (8, 8) (16, 16, 16) rows—10 (14, 18) (16, 20, 24) sts when all bind-offs have been completed.
Bind off.

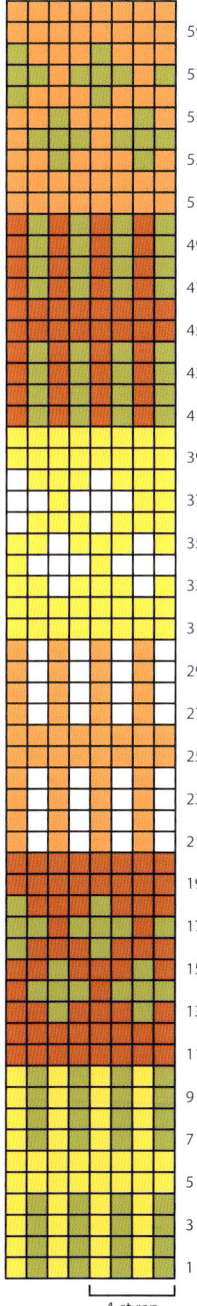

Chart (Child sizes)

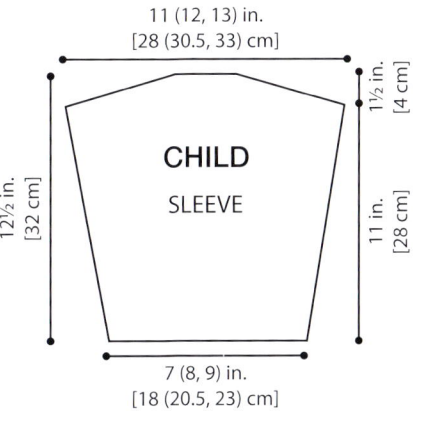

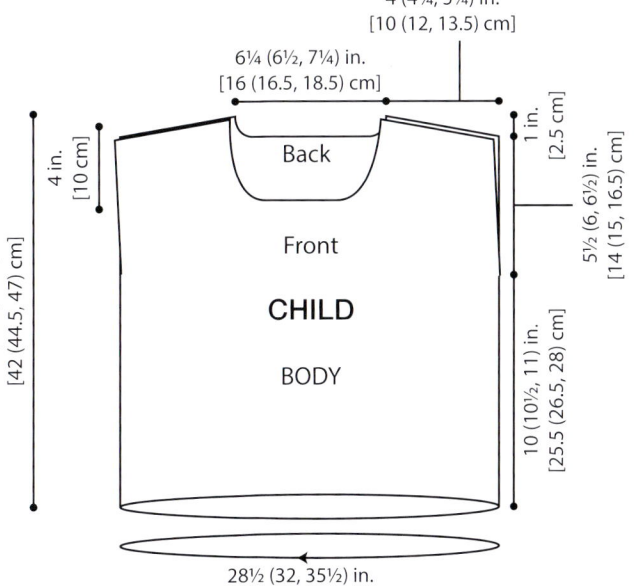

Mother and Child Pullovers

FINISHING

Sew shoulder seams.

Neckband

From RS with shorter needle and A, beg at right shoulder seam, pick up and k 5 sts down right back neck edge, 22 (24, 26) (32, 34, 36) back neck sts from holder, 5 sts up left back neck edge to left shoulder seam, 20 sts down left front edge, 12 (14, 16) (22, 24, 26) front neck sts from holder, and 20 sts up right front edge—84 (88, 92) (104, 108, 112) sts.

Place marker for beg of rnd. Join by working first st on left-hand needle with working yarn from right-hand needle.

Work K1, p1 Rib worked in rnds for 5 (5, 5) (7, 7, 7) rnds. Bind off.

Sew Sleeve seams. Sew Sleeves into armholes.
Weave in ends. •

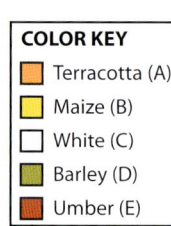

COLOR KEY
- Terracotta (A)
- Maize (B)
- White (C)
- Barley (D)
- Umber (E)

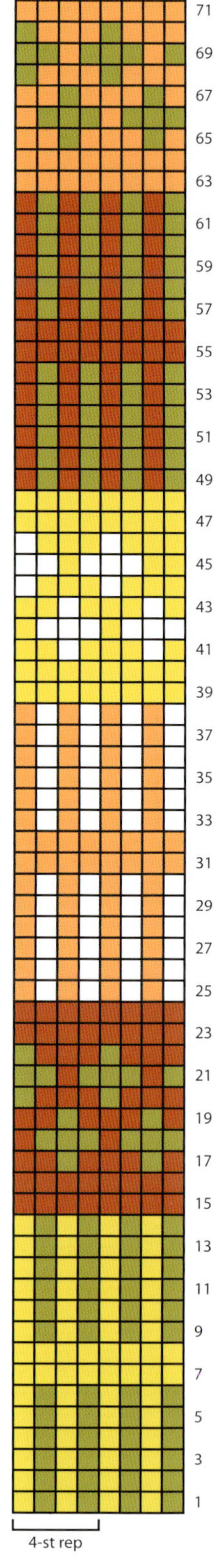

Chart (Adult sizes)

4-st rep

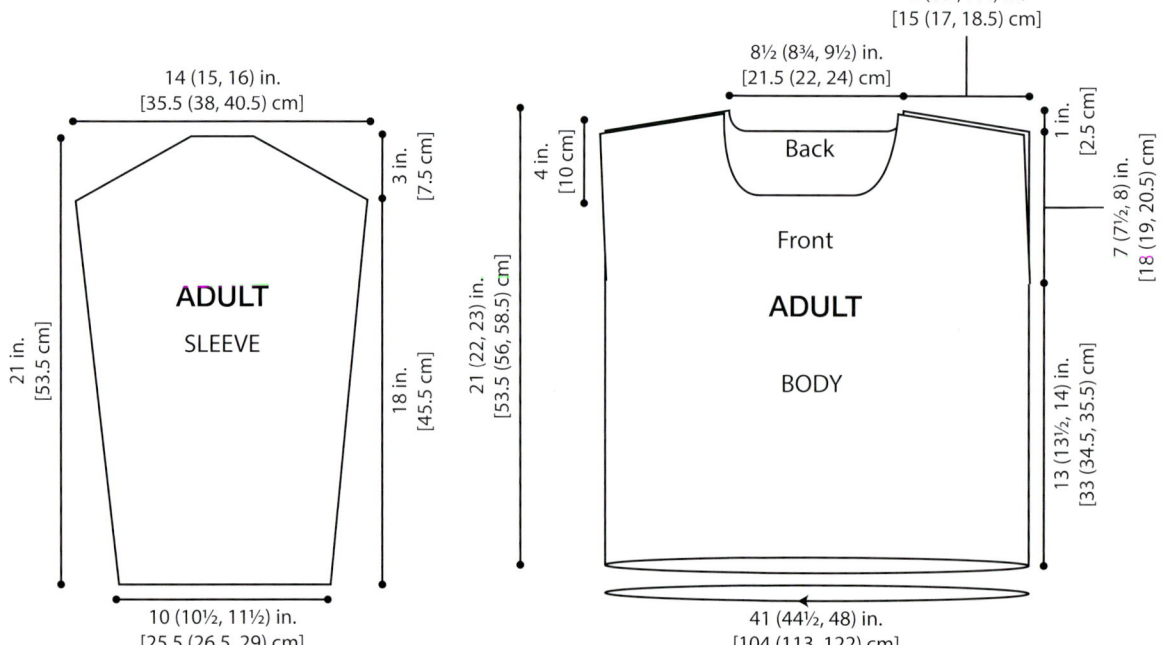

Boxy Cropped Pullover

Easy

SIZES
S/L (1X/2X).

MEASUREMENTS
Finished Bust About 56 (64)"/142 (162.5)
Finished Length About 18 (19)"/45.5 (48.5)cm

MATERIALS
YARN
LION BRAND® Homespun®, 6oz/170g balls, each approx 185yd/169m (acrylic/polyester)
• 3 (4) balls in #318 Sierra

KNITTING NEEDLES
• One size 10½ (6.5mm) circular needle, 16"/40.5cm long, *or size to obtain gauge*
• One size 10½ (6.5mm) circular needle, 36"/91.5cm long

NOTIONS
• Stitch markers
• Tapestry needle

GAUGE
12 sts + 17 rows = about 4"/10cm in St st.
BE SURE TO CHECK YOUR GAUGE.

PATTERN STITCH
K1, P1 RIB WORKED IN ROWS
(over an even number of sts)
Row 1 (RS) *K1, p1; rep from * to end of row.
Row 2 K the knit sts and p the purl sts.
Rep Row 2 for K1, p1 Rib worked in rows.

NOTES
1) Pullover is worked in 4 pieces: Back, Front, and 2 Sleeves.
2) A circular needle is used to accommodate the number of sts. Work back and forth in rows on the circular needle as if working on straight needles.
3) The shorter circular needle is used to work the turtleneck in the round.

PULLOVER
BACK
With longer needle, cast on 84 (96) sts.
Beg with Row 1 (RS) of pattern, work in K1, p1 Rib for 4 rows.

Boxy Cropped Pullover

Beg with a RS (knit) row, work in St st (k on RS, p on WS) until piece measures about 15 (16)"/38 (40.5)cm from beg, end with a WS row as the last row you work.

Shape shoulders
Row 1 (RS) Bind off 4 (5) sts, k to end of row—80 (91) sts.
Row 2 Bind off 4 (5) sts, p to end of row—76 (86) sts.
Rows 3–12 Rep Rows 1 and 2 for 5 more times—36 sts.
Row 13 Bind off 4 (3) sts, k to end of row—32 (33) sts.
Row 14 Bind off 4 (3) sts, p to end of row—28 (30) sts.
Place rem sts onto the shorter needle and set aside.

FRONT
Make same as Back.
Place rem sts of Front onto the shorter needle with the rem sts from the Back, with the RS of both the Front and Back facing.

TURTLENECK
Place marker for beg of rnd. Join by working the first st on the left hand needle with the working yarn from the right hand needle—you'll have 56 (60) sts.
Work in St st worked in rnds (k every st in every rnd) for about 9"/23cm.
Bind off loosely.

SLEEVES (MAKE 2)
With longer needle, cast on 28 (32) sts.
Beg with Row 1 of pattern, work in K1, p1 Rib for 6 rows.

Inc Row (RS) K1, kfb, k to last 2 sts, kfb, k1—30 (34) sts.
Beg with a WS (purl) row, work in St st for 11 (9) rows.
Rep Inc Row—32 (36) sts.
Rep last 12 (10) rows for 2 (3) more times—36 (42) sts when all inc have been completed.

Work even in St st until piece measures about 12½"/32cm from beg.
Bind off.

FINISHING
Sew shoulder seams.
Place markers on both sides of Back and Front, about 6 (7)"/15 (18)cm below shoulder seams. Sew tops of Sleeves between markers.
Sew side and Sleeve seams.

Weave in ends. •

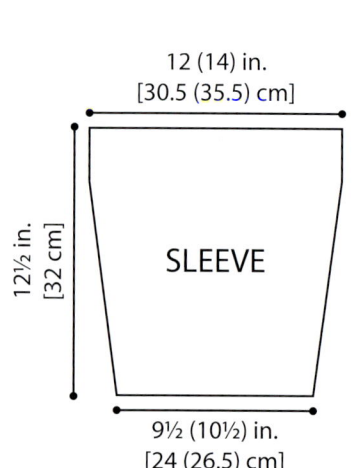

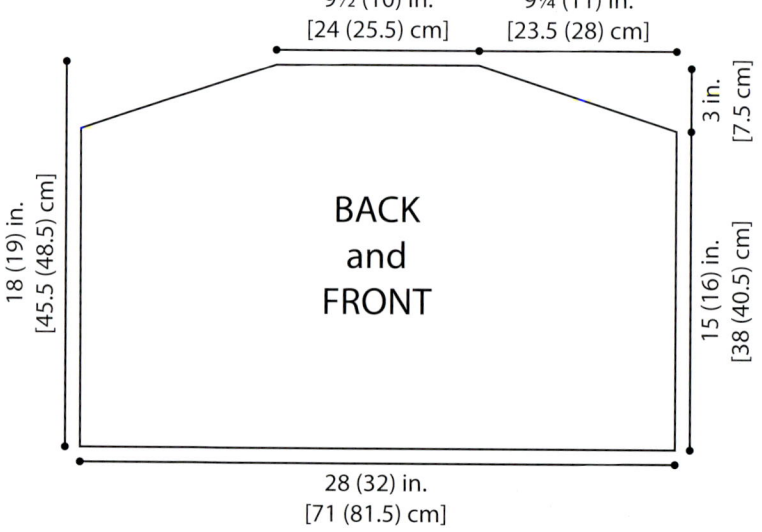

Exaggerated Raglan Pullover

Easy

SIZES
S/M (L/1X).

MEASUREMENTS
Finished Bust About 60 (70)"/152.5 (178)cm
Finished Center Front Length, excluding collar About 26½ (29½)"/67.5 (75)cm

MATERIALS
YARN
LION BRAND® Wool-Ease® Thick & Quick®, 6oz/170g balls, each approx 106yd/97m (acrylic/wool)
• 8 (11) balls in #135 Spice

KNITTING NEEDLES
• One size 13 (9mm) circular needle, 16"/40.5cm long, *or size to obtain gauge*
• One size 13 (9mm) circular needle, 24"/61cm long
• One size 13 (9mm) circular needle, 40"/101.5cm long
• One set (5) of size 13 (9mm) double-pointed needles

NOTIONS
• Stitch markers
• Stitch holders
• Tapestry needle

GAUGE
9½ sts + 13 rnds = about 4"/10cm in St st.
BE SURE TO CHECK YOUR GAUGE.

PATTERN STITCHES
K1, P1 RIB WORKED IN RNDS
(worked over an even number of sts)
Rnd 1 *K1, p1; rep from * to end of rnd.
Rnd 2 K the knit sts and p the purl sts.
Rep Rnd 2 for K1, p1 Rib worked in rnds.

NOTES
1) Pullover is worked in the round from the top down.
2) At underarms, work is divided and body and sleeves worked separately.
3) Markers are placed to indicate increase locations for raglans and at center front and back. Use one color markers for raglans and different color markers for center front and back.
4) The ribbed neck is worked from sts picked up around the neck edge of the Pullover.

PULLOVER
With middle length circular needle, cast on 68 sts. Place marker for beg of rnd. Join by working first st on left-hand needle with working yarn from right-hand needle and being careful not to twist sts.
Note When you pm on next rnd, use different color markers for raglans and for center front and back.
Set-Up Rnd 1 (RS) K8, pm for raglan, k1, p2, k1, pm for raglan; k7, pm for center front, k1, p2, k1, pm for center front; k7, pm for raglan, k1, p2, k1, pm for raglan, k8, pm for raglan, k1, p2, k1, pm for raglan; k7, pm for center back, k1, p2, k1, pm for center back; k7, pm for raglan, k1, p2, k1, use beg of rnd marker as final raglan marker.
Rnds 2 and 3 *K to marker, sm, k1, p2, k1, sm; rep from * around.
Rnd 4 (Raglan Inc) M1, k to first (raglan) marker, M1, sm, k1, p2, k1, sm, M1, k to next (front) marker, sm, k1, p2, k1, sm, [k to next (raglan) marker, M1, sm, k1, p2, k1, sm, M1] twice, k to next (back) marker, sm, k1, p2, k1, sm, k to next (raglan) marker, M1, sm, k1, p2, k1, sm—76 sts.
Rnd 5 *K to marker, sm, k1, p2, k1, sm; rep from * around.

Exaggerated Raglan Pullover

Inc Rnd 6 *M1, k to marker, M1, sm, k1, p2, k1, sm; rep from * around—88 sts.

Rnd 7 *K to marker, sm, k1, p2, k1, sm; rep from * around.

Note Change to longer circular needle as needed.

Rnds 8–15 Rep Rnds 4–7 for 2 more times—128 sts.

Rnd 16 Rep Rnd 4—136 sts.

Rnds 17 and 18 Rep Rnd 5 twice.

Rnd 19 Rep Rnd 4—144 sts.

Rnd 20 Rep Rnd 5.

Rnd 21 (Center Front/Back Inc) K to first marker, sm, k1, p2, k1, sm, k to next (front) marker, M1, sm, k1, p2, k1, sm, M1, [k to next marker, sm, k1, p2, k1, sm] twice, k to next marker (back), M1, sm, k1, p2, k1, sm, M1, k to next marker, sm, k1, p2, k1—148 sts.

Rnd 22 Rep Rnd 4—156 sts.

Rnds 23–25 Rep Rnds 17–19—164 sts in Rnd 25.

Rnds 26 and 27 Rep Rnd 5 twice.

Rnd 28 Rep Rnd 6—176 sts.

Rnds 29–31 Rep Rnds 17–19—184 sts in Rnd 31.

Rnds 32–34 Rep Rnds 17–19—192 sts in Rnd 34.

Rnd 35 Rep Rnd 21—196 sts.

Rnd 36 Rep Rnd 5.

Rnd 37 Rep Rnd 4—204 sts.

Rnds 38–40 Rep Rnds 17–19—212 sts in Rnd 40.

Rnd 41 Rep Rnd 5.

Rnd 42 Rep Rnd 21—216 sts.

Rnds 43–47 (58) Rep Rnds 16–20 (31)—232 (272) sts in last rnd worked.

DIVIDE FOR BODY AND SLEEVES

Next Rnd *K to marker, sm, k1, p2, k1, sm; rep from * for 4 more times, k to next marker, sm, k1, p2 (you should be 1 st from beg of rnd marker), place next 44 (52) sts on holder for first sleeve, pm for side seam and new beg of rnd marker.

Next Rnd P2, k1, remove marker, k to next marker, sm, k1, p2, k1, sm, k to next marker, remove marker, k1, p2, pm for side seam, place next 44 (52) sts on holder for 2nd sleeve, p2, k1, remove marker, k to next marker, sm, k1, p2, k1, sm, k to next marker, remove marker, k1, p2, sm—you should have 44 (52) sts on each of 2 holders for sleeves and 144 (168) sts rem on needle for body.

BODY

Rnd 1 P2, k to next (front) marker, sm, k1, p2, k1, sm, k to 2 sts before next (side) marker, p2, sm, p2, k to next marker, sm, k1, p2, k1, sm, k to last 2 sts, p2, sm.

Rnd 2 (Center Front/Back Inc) P2, k to next marker, M1, sm, k1, p2, k1, sm, M1, k to 2 sts before next marker, p2, sm, p2, k to next marker, M1, sm, k1, p2, k1, sm, M1, k to last 2 sts, p2, sm—148 (172) sts.

Rnds 3–5 P2, k to next marker, sm, k1, p2, k1, sm, k to 2 sts before next marker, p2, sm, p2, k to next marker, sm, k1, p2, k1, sm, k to last 2 sts, p2, sm.

Rnd 6 (Center Front/Back Inc, Side Seam Dec) K2tog, k to next marker, M1, sm, k1, p2, k1, sm, M1, k to 2 sts before next marker, k2tog tbl, sm, k2tog, k to next marker, M1, sm, k1, p2, k1, sm, M1, k to last 2 sts, k2tog tbl, sm—148 (172) sts.

Rnds 7–9 K to next marker, sm, k1, p2, k1, sm, k to next marker, sm, k to next marker, sm, k1, p2, k1, sm, k to end of rnd, sm.

Rnd 10 (Center Front/Back Inc) K to next marker, M1, sm, k1, p2, k1, sm, M1, k to next marker, sm, k to next marker, M1, sm, k1, p2, k1, sm, M1, k to end of rnd, sm—152 (176) sts.

Rnd 11 Rep Rnd 7.

Rnd 12 (Side Seam Dec) K2tog, k to next marker, sm, k1, p2, k1, sm, k to 2 sts before next marker, k2tog tbl, sm, k2tog, k to next marker, sm, k1, p2, k1, sm, k to last 2 sts, k2tog tbl, sm—148 (172) sts.

Rnd 13 Rep Rnd 7.

Rnd 14 Rep Rnd 10—152 (176) sts.

Rnds 15–17 Rep Rnd 7.

Rnds 18–29 Rep Rnds 6–17—156 (180) sts when all inc and dec completed.

Rnds 30–33 Rep Rnds 6–9.

Rnd 34 Rep Rnd 7.

Lower Ribbing

Remove side seam marker as you work Rnd 1.

Set-up Rnd 1 *K2tog, p1, [k1, p1] to next marker,

remove marker, k1, M1P, pm, k2tog, pm, M1P, k1, remove marker, p1, [k1, p1] to next marker; rep from * once more—156 (180) sts.

Rnd 2 Work in K1, p1 Rib and sm as you come to them.

Rnd 3 (Center Front/Back Inc) *Work in K1, p1 Rib to next marker, M1, sm, k1, sm, M1; rep from * once more, work in K1, p1 Rib to end of rnd—160 (184) sts.

Rnd 4 *Work in K1, p1 Rib to 1 st before next marker, p1, sm, k1, sm, p1; rep from * once more.

Rnd 5 (Center Front/Back Inc) *Work in K1, p1 Rib to 1 st before next marker, k1, M1P, sm, k1, sm, M1P, k1; rep from * once more, work in K1, p1 Rib to end of rnd—164 (188) sts.

Next Rnd Work in K1, p1 Rib around, removing front and back markers as you come to them.

Last 2 Rnds Work in K1, p1 Rib.

Bind off in rib.

SLEEVES

Place 44 (52) sts of one sleeve onto shorter circular needle. Place marker for beg of rnd. Join by working first st on left-hand needle with working yarn from right-hand needle.

Rnds 1 and 2 Knit.

Dec Rnd 3 K1, k2tog tbl, k to 2 sts before end of rnd, k2tog—42 (50) sts.

Rep Rnds 1–3 for 5 (6) more times—32 (38) sts, changing to double-pointed needles when sts have dec sufficiently.

Cuff ribbing

Set-Up Rnd 1 *K1, p2tog; rep from * to last 2 sts, k1, p1—22 (26) sts.

Work in K1, p1 Rib for 6 rnds. Bind off in rib.

Rep for 2nd sleeve.

FINISHING

Ribbed neck

From RS with shorter circular needle, pick up and k 56 sts evenly spaced around neck edge. Join by working first st on left-hand needle with working yarn from right-hand needle.

Work in K1, p1 Rib for about 2¾"/7cm. Bind off in rib.

Sew underarms closed.

Weave in ends. •

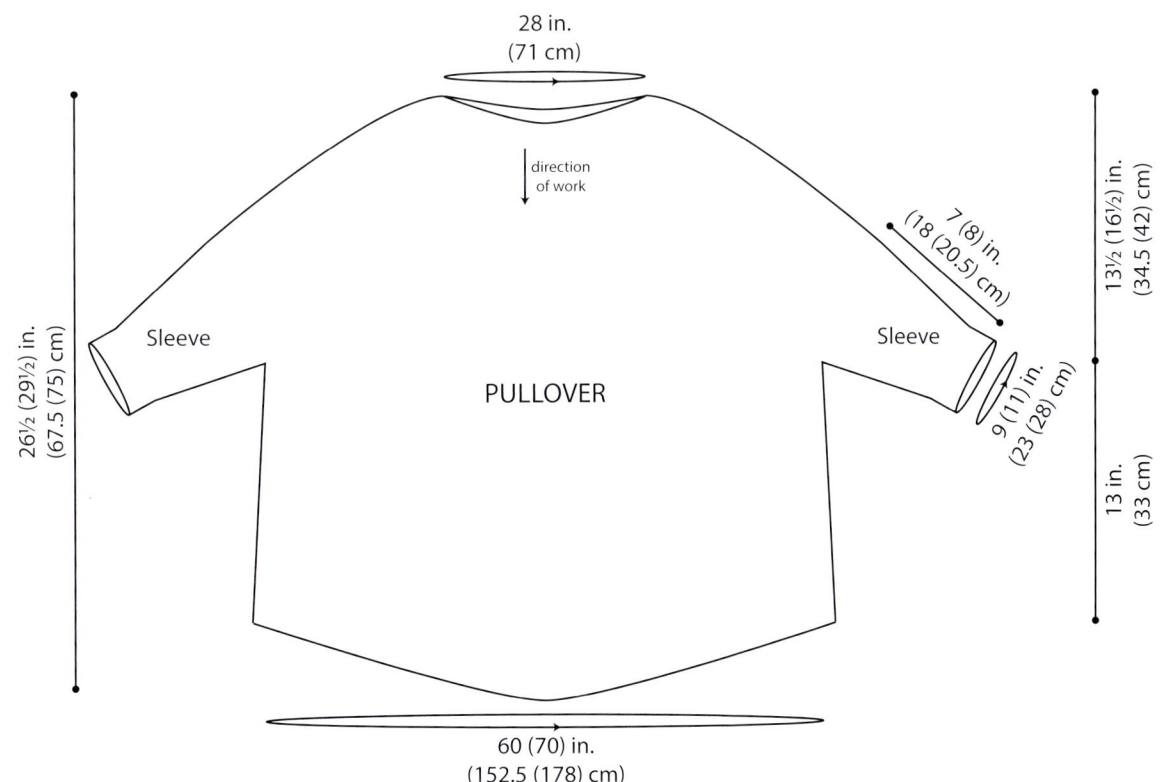

Folke Pullover

Easy

SIZES
S (M/L, 1X/2X).

MEASUREMENTS
Finished Bust About 46 (52, 58)"/117 (132, 147.5)cm
Finished Length About 18½ (19½, 20½)"/47 (49.5, 52)cm

MATERIALS
YARN

LION BRAND® Wool-Ease® Thick & Quick®, 6oz/170g balls, each approx 106yd/97m (acrylic/wool)
- 3 (4, 5) balls in #124 Barley (A)
- 1 (2, 2) ball(s) each in #143 Claret (B), #138 Cranberry (C), #153 Black (D), and #099 Fisherman (E)

KNITTING NEEDLES
- One size 13 (9mm) circular needle, 16"/40.5cm long, *or size to obtain gauge*
- One size 13 (9mm) circular needle, 24"/61cm long
- One size 13 (9mm) circular needle, 36"/91.5cm long
- One size 13 (9mm) circular needle, 40"/101.5cm long

NOTIONS
- Stitch markers
- Stitch holders
- Tapestry needle

GAUGE
8 sts = about 4"/10cm in St st worked in the rnd.
BE SURE TO CHECK YOUR GAUGE.

CABLE CAST ON
*Insert right needle between first 2 sts on left needle, wrap yarn and pull through (as if knitting a st), transfer new st to left needle; rep from * for desired number of sts.

NOTES
1) Pullover is worked in one piece, in the round, beginning at neck.
2) At underarms, piece is divided, then body and sleeves are worked separately. The body is worked in the round. The sleeves are worked back and forth in rows.
3) Stranded colorwork on the Pullover uses 2 colors on each round or row. Carry unused color loosely across WS of piece.

PULLOVER
YOKE

With shortest circular needle and A, cast on 44 (48, 52) sts. Place marker for beg of rnd. Join by working the first st on the left hand needle with the working yarn from the right hand needle and being careful not to twist sts.
Knit 4 rnds.
Next Rnd *K11 (12, 13), M1; rep from * 3 more times—you will have 48 (52, 56) sts in this rnd.

Begin colorwork
Note Change to longer and longer circular needles as sts are increased and no longer fit comfortably on a shorter needle.
Rnd 1 With A, k1, *with B, k1; with A, k3; rep from * to last 3 sts, with B, k1; with A, k2.
Rnd 2 *With B, k3; with A, k1; rep from * around.
Rnd 3 Rep Rnd 1.

Folke Pullover

Inc Rnd 4 *With C, k3; with A, k1, M1; rep from * around—60 (65, 70) sts.

Rnds 5 and 6 *With C, k3; with A, k2; rep from * around.

Inc Rnd 7 With A, k4, *M1, k5; rep from * to last st, M1, k1—72 (78, 84) sts.

Rnd 8 With A, k1, *with D, k1; with A, k5; rep from * to last 5 sts, with D, k1; with A, k4.

Rnd 9 *With D, k3; with A, k3; rep from * around.

Rnd 10 With D, k4, *with A, k1; with D, k5; rep from * to last 2 sts, with A, k1; with D, k1.

Inc Rnd 11 With D, k5, *M1, k6; rep from * to last st, M1, k1—84 (91, 98) sts.

Rnd 12 With D, k1, *with B, k1; with D, k6; rep from * to last 6 sts, with B, k1; with D, k5.

Rnd 13 *With B, k3; with D, k4; rep from * around.

Rnd 14 With B, k4, *with D, k2; with B, k5; rep from * to last 3 sts, with D, k2; with B, k1.

Inc Rnd 15 With B, k1, *with A, k1; with B, k3; with A, M1; with B, k3; rep from * to last 6 sts, with A, k1; with B, k3; with A, M1; with B, k2—96 (104, 112) sts.

Rnd 16 *With A, k3; with B, k1; rep from * around.

Rnd 17 *With E, k1; with A, k1; rep from * around.

Rnd 18 *With A, k1; with E, k1; rep from * around.

Inc Rnd 19 *With C, k8 (6, 5), M1; rep from * 11 (15, 19) more times, k to end of rnd—108 (120, 132) sts.

Rnds 20 and 21 *With B, k2; with C, k2; rep from * around.

Rnds 22 and 23 With A, k1; *with D, k4; with A, k2; rep from * to last 5 sts, with D, k4; with A, k1.

Rnds 24 and 25 With A, k2, *with D, k2; with A, k4; rep from * to last 4 sts, with D, k2; with A, k2.

Rnds 26 and 27 With A, k1, *with E, k4; with A, k2; rep from * to last 5 sts, with E, k4; with A, k1.

Inc Rnd 28 *With A, k9 (10, 11), M1; rep from * around—120 (132, 144) sts.

Rnd 29 With A, k1, *with C, k1; with A, k3; rep from * to last 3 sts, with C, k1; with A, k2.

Rnd 30 *With C, k3; with A, k1; rep from * around.

Rnd 31 Rep Rnd 29.

Rnds 32–34 *With B, k3; with A, k1; rep from * around.

FOR SIZE S ONLY

Cut B and C.

Proceed to Divide for Body and Sleeves.

FOR SIZE M/L ONLY

Rnds 35–37 Rep Rnds 29–31.

Cut B and C.

Proceed to Divide for Body and Sleeves.

FOR SIZE 1X/2X ONLY

Rnds 35–40 Rep Rnds 29–34.

Cut B and C.

Proceed to Divide for Body and Sleeves.

DIVIDE FOR BODY AND SLEEVES

Dividing Rnd Place first 20 (22, 24) sts onto a holder for first sleeve; with A, cable cast on 6 (8, 10) sts for underarm, k40 (44, 48), place next 20 (22, 24) sts onto a holder for 2nd sleeve, cable cast on 6 (8, 10) sts for underarm, k40 (44, 48)—92 (104, 116) sts on needle for body. Place marker for beg of rnd and join to work in the rnd.

BODY

Rnd 1 *With A, k1; with D, k1; rep from * around.
Rnd 2 *With D, k1; with A, k1; rep from * around.
Rnd 3 With A, knit.
Rnd 4 With A, k1, *with E, k1; with A, k3; rep from * to last 3 sts, with E, k1; with A, k2.
Rnd 5 *With E, k3; with A, k1; rep from * around.
Rnd 6 Rep Rnd 4.
Cut D and E. Continue with A only.
Rnd 7 Knit.

Ribbing

Rnds 8–15 *K1, p1; rep from * around.
Bind off in rib.

SLEEVES

Note Work back and forth in rows on the circular needle as if working on straight needles.
Slip 20 (22, 24) sleeve sts from one holder onto shortest circular needle.
Row 1 (RS) From RS with A, cable cast-on 4 (5, 6) sts, k the sts just cast on, k20 (22, 24) sleeve sts—24 (27, 30) sts.
Row 2 With A, cable cast on 4 (5, 6) sts, p the sts just cast on, p to end of row—28 (32, 36) sts.
Row 3 *With A, k1; with D, k1; rep from * across.
Row 4 *With D, p1; with A, p1; rep from * across.
Row 5 With A, knit.
Row 6 With A, p1, *with E, p1; with A, p3; rep from * to last 3 sts, with E, p1; with A, p2.
Row 7 *With E, k3; with A, k1; rep from * across.
Row 8 Rep Rnd 4.
Cut B, D, and E. Continue with A only.
Row 9 With A, knit.

Ribbing

Row 10 (WS) *K1, p1; rep from * across.
Dec Row 11 P1, k2tog, k the knit sts and p the purl sts to last 3 sts, p2tog, k1—26 (30, 34) sts.
Rows 12–16 K the knit sts and p the purl sts.
Dec Row 17 K1, p2tog, k the knit sts and p the purl sts to last 3 sts, k2tog, p1—24 (28, 32) sts.
Rows 18–22 Rep Rows 12–16.
Row 23 Rep Row 11—22 (26, 30) sts.
Row 24 K the knit sts and p the purl sts.
Rep Row 24 until sleeve measures about 14 (15, 16)"/35.5 (38, 40.5)cm from underarm.
Bind off in rib.
Rep for 2nd sleeve.

FINISHING

Sew sleeve and underarm seams.
Weave in ends. •

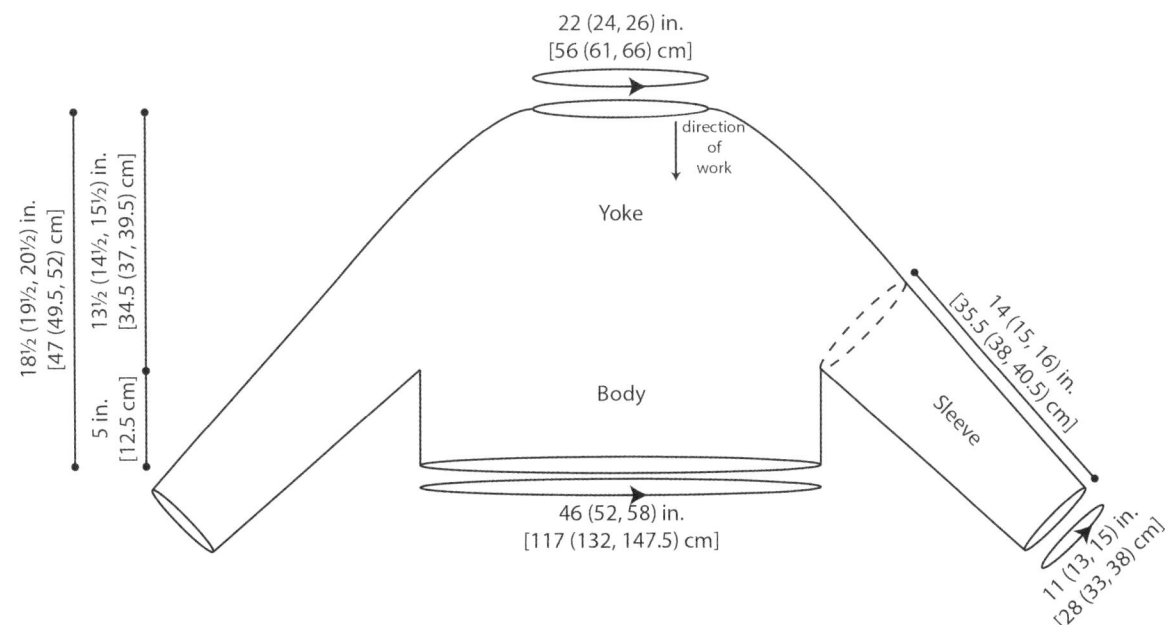

Doreen Striped Pullover

Easy

SIZES
S (M, L, 1X, 2X, 3X).

MEASUREMENTS
Finished Bust About 44 (48, 52, 55, 58, 62)"/112 (122, 132, 139.5, 147.5, 157.5)cm
Finished Length About 21 (21, 22, 22, 23, 23)"/53.5 (53.5, 56, 56, 58.5, 58.5)cm

MATERIALS
YARN
LION BRAND® Touch of Merino, 3½oz/100g balls, each approx 257yd/235m (acrylic, merino wool)
- 3 (4, 4, 4, 5, 5) balls in #150 Oxford Grey (A)
- 1 (1, 1, 1, 1, 1) ball each in #105 Swedish Blue (B), #172 Ivy (C), #133 Amberglow (D), and #113 Beet Red (E)

KNITTING NEEDLES
- One size 6 (4mm) circular needle, 16"/40.5cm long, *or size to obtain gauge*
- One size 6 (4mm) circular needle, 29"/73.5cm long

NOTIONS
- Stitch markers
- Tapestry needle

GAUGE
22 sts + 30 rows = about 4"/10cm in St st.
BE SURE TO CHECK YOUR GAUGE.

PATTERN STITCHES
K1, P1 RIB WORKED IN ROWS
(worked over an even number of sts)
Row 1 *K1, p1; rep from * to end of row.
Row 2 K the knit sts and p the purl sts.
Rep Row 2 for K1, p1 Rib worked in rows.

K1, P1 RIB WORKED IN RNDS
(worked over an even number of sts)
Rnd 1 *K1, p1; rep from * to end of rnd.
Rep Rnd 1 for K1, p1 Rib worked in rnds.

NOTES
1) Pullover is worked in 4 pieces: Back, Front, and 2 Sleeves.
2) Each piece begins with ribbing and then is worked in St st stripes.
3) Work neckband from sts picked up around neck edge.
4) A longer circular needle is used to accommodate the number of sts. Work back and forth on the circular needle as if working on straight needles.

STRIPE SEQUENCE
Work 4 rows with B, 8 rows with A, 4 rows with C, 8 rows with A, 4 rows with D, 8 rows with A, 4 rows with E, and 8 rows with A; rep these 48 rows for Stripe Sequence.

PULLOVER
BACK
With longer needle and A, cast on 122 (134, 144, 152, 160, 172) sts.
Work in K1, p1 Rib worked in rows until piece measures about 1½"/4cm from beg, end with a WS row as the last row you work.

Work in St st (k on RS, p on WS) until piece measures about 3½ (3½, 4½, 4½, 5½, 5½)"/9 (9, 11.5, 11.5, 14, 14)cm from beg, end with a WS row as last row you work.

Striped section

Continue in St st and change yarn color by following the 48-row Stripe Sequence twice for a total of 96 rows.

Continue with A only.
Work even in St st until piece measures about 19 (19, 20, 20, 21, 21)"/48.5 (48.5, 51, 51, 53.5, 53.5)cm from beg, end with a WS row as the last row you work.

Shape neck

Row 1 (RS) K43 (49, 53, 57, 59, 65) for right side; join a 2nd ball of yarn and bind off center 36 (36, 38, 38, 42, 42) sts for back neck; k to end of row for left side—you will have 43 (49, 53, 57, 59, 65) sts on each side.
You will now work both sides AT THE SAME TIME with separate balls of yarn.
Row 2 Purl across all sts of both sides using separate balls of yarn.
Dec Row 3 On right side, k to last 3 sts, ssk, k1; on left side, k1, k2tog, k to end—42 (48, 52, 56, 58, 64) sts on each side.
Rows 4–9 Rep Rows 2 and 3 for 3 more times—39 (45, 49, 53, 55, 61) sts on each side when all dec have been completed.
Work even in St st on each side with separate balls of yarn until piece measures about 21 (21, 22, 22, 23, 23)"/53.5 (53.5, 56, 56, 58.5, 58.5)cm from beg.
Bind off all sts on both sides using separate balls of yarn.

FRONT

Cast on and work same as Back until piece measures about 17 (17, 18, 18, 19, 19)"/43 (43, 45.5, 45.5, 48.5, 48.5)cm from beg and striped section is complete, end with a WS row as the last row you work.

Shape neck

Row 1 (RS) K51 (57, 61, 65, 67, 73) for left side; join a 2nd ball of yarn and bind off center 20 (20, 22, 22, 26,

Doreen Striped Pullover

26) sts for front neck; k to end of row for right side—51 (57, 61, 65, 67, 73) sts on each side.

You will now work both sides AT THE SAME TIME with separate balls of yarn.

Row 2 On right side, p to end; on left side, bind off 4 sts, p to end.

Row 3 On left side, k to end; on right side, bind off 4 sts, k to end—47 (53, 57, 61, 63, 69) sts on each side.

Row 4 On right side, p to end; on left side, bind off 3 sts, p to end.

Row 5 On left side, k to end; on right side, bind off 3 sts, k to end—44 (50, 54, 58, 60, 66) sts on each side.

Row 6 On right side, p to end; on left side, bind off 2 sts, p to end.

Row 7 On left side, k to end; on right side, bind off 2 sts, k to end—42 (48, 52, 56, 58, 64) sts on each side.

Row 8 On right side, p to end; on left side, p to end.

Row 9 On left side, k to last 3 sts, ssk, k1; on right side, k1, k2tog, k to end—41 (47, 51, 55, 57, 63) sts on each side.

Rows 10–13 Rep Rows 8 and 9 for 2 more times—39 (45, 49, 53, 55, 61) sts on each side when all dec have been completed.

Work even in St st on each side with separate balls of yarn until piece measures same as Back.

Bind off all sts on both sides using separate balls of yarn.

SLEEVES (MAKE 2)

With longer needle and A, cast on 56 (58, 62, 64, 66, 70) sts.

Work in K1, p1 Rib worked in rows until piece measures about 1½"/4cm from beg, end with a RS row as the last row you work.

Note Sleeve inc and color changes for striped section are worked AT THE SAME TIME. Work inc as instructed and when Sleeve is about 3½"/9cm long you change yarn colors to follow Stripe Sequence while continuing to work inc.

Striped section and sleeve shaping

Work even in St st for 3 (1, 1, 1, 1, 1) row(s).

Inc Row (RS) K2, M1L, k to last 2 sts, M1R, k2—58 (60, 64, 66, 68, 72) sts.

Rep last 4 (2, 2, 2, 2, 2) rows for 1 (1, 1, 5, 7, 7) more times—60 (62, 66, 76, 82, 86) sts when all inc have been completed.

Work even in St st for 3 rows.

Rep Inc Row—62 (64, 68, 78, 84, 88) sts.

Rep last 4 rows for 11 (12, 13, 11, 11, 11) more times—84 (88, 94, 100, 106, 110) sts when all inc have been completed.

Continue with A only.

Work even in St st until piece measures about 11 (11, 11½, 11½, 12, 12)"/28 (28, 29, 29, 30.5, 30.5)cm from beg.

Bind off.

FINISHING

Sew shoulder seams.

Neckband

From RS with shorter needle and A, beg at left shoulder seam, pick up and k 126 (126, 130, 130, 138, 138) sts evenly spaced around neck edge. Place marker for beg of rnd. Join by working first st on left needle with working yarn from right needle.

Work in K1, p1 Rib worked in rnds for ¾"/2cm. Bind off loosely.

Place markers on side edges of Front and Back about 7½ (8, 8½, 9, 9½, 10)"/19 (20.5, 21.5, 23, 24, 25.5)cm below shoulder seams. Sew tops of Sleeves between markers. Sew side and Sleeve seams.

Weave in ends. •

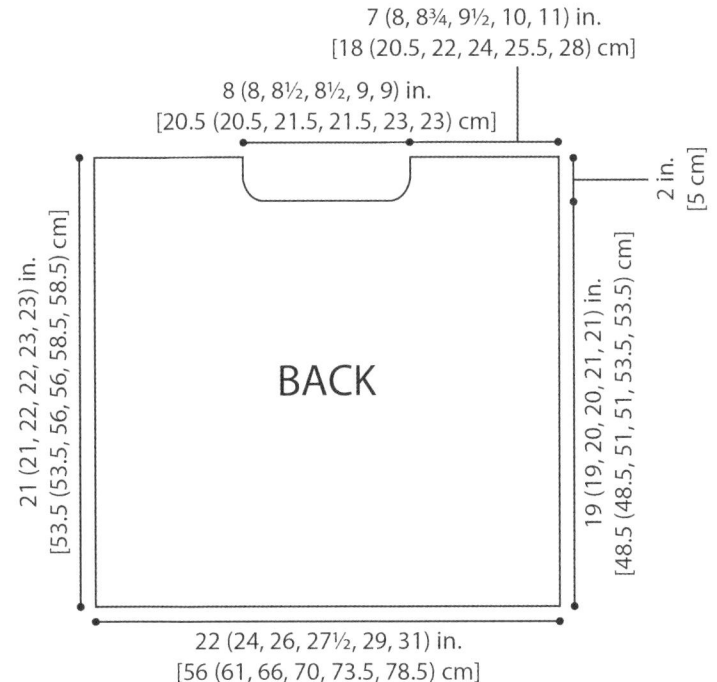

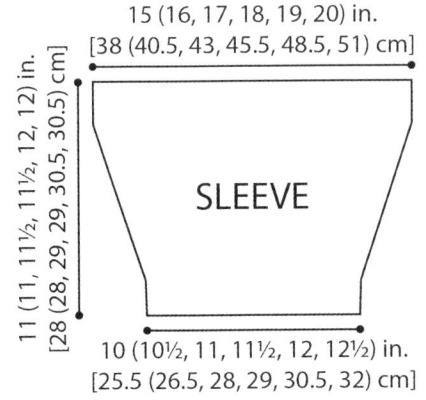

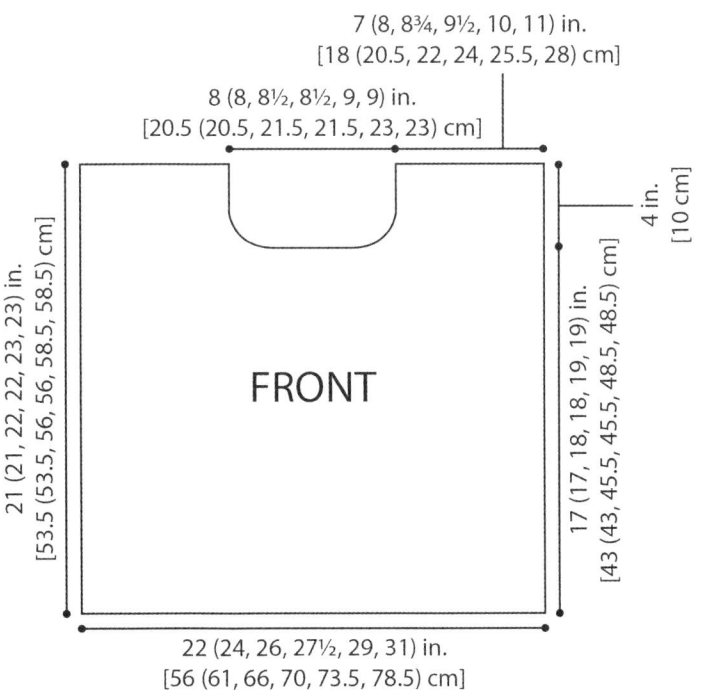

Essential Fall Pullover

Intermediate

SIZES
S (M, L, 1X, 2X, 3X).

MEASUREMENTS
Finished Bust 38 (42, 46, 50, 54, 58)"/96.5 (106.5, 117, 127, 137, 147.5)cm

Finished Length 25½ (26, 26½, 27½, 28, 28½)"/65 (66, 67.5, 69, 71, 72.5)cm

MATERIALS
YARN
LION BRAND® Heartland®, 5oz/142g balls, each approx 251yd/230m (acrylic/rayon)

- 3 (3, 3, 4, 4, 5) balls in #369 Shenandoah Tweed (A)
- 1 (1, 2, 2, 2, 3) balls in #350 Mount Rainier Tweed (B)
- 2 (2, 2, 3, 3, 3) balls in #353 Black Canyon Tweed (C)

KNITTING NEEDLES
- One pair size 7 (4.5mm) knitting needles, *or size to obtain gauge*
- One pair size 5 (3.75mm) knitting needles
- One size 5 (3.75mm) circular needle, 16"/40.5cm long

NOTIONS
- Removable stitch markers
- Tapestry needle

GAUGE
18 sts + 24 rows = 4"/10cm in St st with larger needles.
BE SURE TO CHECK YOUR GAUGE.

NOTES
1) Pullover is worked in 6 pieces, Back, Front, 2 Side Panels, and 2 Sleeves.
2) For sizes S and M, wind a 2nd ball of B before beginning.
3) End with a WS row means that the last row you work should be a WS row, and the next row that you are ready to work will be a RS row.
4) When you see '—12 sts' in the instructions, this lets you know how many sts you will have at the end of that specific row.

PATTERN STITCHES
K1, P1 RIB OVER AN ODD NUMBER OF STS
Row 1 K1, *p1, k1; rep from * to end of row.
Row 2 K the knit sts and p the purl sts.
Rep Row 2 for K1, p1 rib over an odd number of sts.

K1, P1 RIB OVER AN EVEN NUMBER OF STS
Row 1 *K1, p1; rep from * to end of row.
Row 2 K the knit sts and p the purl sts.
Rep Row 2 for K1, p1 rib over an even number of sts.

PULLOVER
BACK
With smaller straight needles and A, cast on 55 (59, 63, 67, 71, 75) sts.
Work K1, p1 Rib until piece measures 2½"/6.5cm from beg.
Change to larger straight needles and, beg with a RS (knit) row, work St st (k on RS, p on WS) for 14 rows.
Inc Row (RS) K2, kfb, k to last 4 sts, kfb, k3—57 (61, 65, 69, 73, 77) sts.
Rep Inc Row every 16th row 4 more times—65 (69, 73, 77, 81, 85) sts when all inc have been completed.
Work St st until piece measures 18½"/47cm from beg, end with a WS row as the last row you work. Place marker on each side edge of last row worked.

Shape Raglan
Dec Row K1, k2tog, k to last 3 sts, SKP, k1—63 (67, 71, 75, 79, 83) sts rem.

Essential Fall Pullover

Next Row Purl.
Rep last 2 rows until 23 sts rem.
Bind off.

FRONT

Work as for Back until 39 sts rem.

Shape Neck

Mark center 13 sts for neck.
Note Work raglan shaping same as for Back, but also work neck shaping AT THE SAME TIME. Read carefully through next section before beginning.
Next Row (RS) K1, k3tog, k to center marked sts, join a 2nd ball of yarn and bind off center 13 sts, k to last 4 sts, SK2P, k1—11 sts rem each side.
Working both sides with separate balls of yarn, work in St st and continue to dec 2 sts at each side edge for raglan and AT THE SAME TIME, work neck shaping by binding off 3 sts from each neck edge once, then 2 sts once—2 sts rem each side after all shaping has been completed. Bind off.

SIDE PANELS (MAKE 2)

With smaller straight needles and B, cast on 24 (28, 32, 36, 40, 46) sts.
Work K1, p1 Rib until piece measures 2½"/6.5cm from beg. Change to larger straight needles and work St st until piece measures 17"/43cm from beg, end with a WS row as the last row you work.

Shape armhole

Mark center 10 (14, 18, 22, 26, 30) sts for armhole.
Row 1 (RS) Work to center marked sts, join a 2nd ball of yarn and bind off center 10 (14, 18, 22, 26, 30) sts, k to end—7 (7, 7, 7, 7, 8) sts rem on each side.
Working both sides AT THE SAME TIME with separate balls of yarn, bind off 2 (2, 2, 2, 2, 3) sts from armhole edge once, then bind off 1 st from each armhole edge 4 times—1 st rem on each side.
Fasten off last st.

LEFT SLEEVE

With smaller straight needles and C, cast on 43 (45, 49, 53, 57, 61) sts.
Work K1, p1 Rib until piece measures 2½"/6.5cm from beg. Change to larger straight needles.
Next Row (RS) K14 (16, 17, 18, 19, 20), M1, k15 (15, 15, 17, 19, 21), M1, k to end—45 (47, 51, 57, 63, 69) sts.
Purl one row.
Next Row K1, M1, k to last st, M1, k1.
Work in St st for 9 rows.
Next Row K1, M1, k to last st, M1, k1.
Rep last 10 rows 7 (8, 8, 9, 9, 9) times more—59 (63, 67, 75, 81, 87) sts.
Continue even (without inc or dec) in St st until piece measures 18"/45.5cm from beg, end with a WS row as the last row you work.

Shape raglans

Bind off 5 (5, 5, 6, 6, 7) sts at beg of next 2 rows, then bind off 4 (4, 4, 5, 6, 6) sts at beg of next 2 rows—41 (45, 49, 53, 57, 61) sts rem.
Dec Row (RS) K1, k2tog, k to last 3 sts, SKP, k1—39 (43, 47, 51, 55, 59) sts rem.
Continue in St st and rep Dec Row every other row 1 (3, 5, 7, 9, 11) more times, then every 4th row 9 times, end with a Dec Row as the last row you work—19 sts rem.

Shape Front Neck

Next Row (WS) Bind off 7 sts, p to end—12 sts rem.
Continue to dec 1 st at beg of RS row every 4th row twice more AT THE SAME TIME, bind off 2 sts from beg of next WS row 4 times.
Bind off rem 2 sts.

RIGHT SLEEVE

Work as for Left Sleeve until 19 sts rem, end with first WS row after Dec Row as the last row you work.

Shape Front Neck

Next Row (RS) Bind off 7 sts, k to end of row—12 sts rem.

Continue to dec 1 st at end of RS row every 4th row twice more AT THE SAME TIME, bind off 2 sts from beg of next RS row 4 times.
Bind off rem 2 sts.

FINISHING

Note When you sew Side Panel to Front and Back, sew the 19"/48.5cm edge of Side Panel to edge of Front/Back shown on schematic as 18½"/47cm long. But, if you lay your pieces out flat, you'll see that the Front/Back edge that you're sewing the Side Panel to is actually longer than 18½"/47cm along the diagonal, so the pieces will fit together!

Sew side edges of Side Panels to Front and Back, aligning top of Side Panel with markers on Front and Back.
Sew Sleeve seams, then sew Sleeves into raglan armholes.

Neckband

From RS with circular needle, join A at right shoulder, pick up and k 20 sts evenly spaced across Back neck, 18 sts along top edge of Sleeve, 28 sts around Front neck, and 18 sts along top of opposite Sleeve—84 sts.
Place marker for beg of rnd and join by knitting first st on left needle with working yarn from right needle.
Purl 1 rnd, knit 1 rnd.
Next Rnd *K1, p1; rep from * around.
Rep last rnd until neckband measures about 1½"/4cm.
Bind off loosely in rib.

Weave in ends.

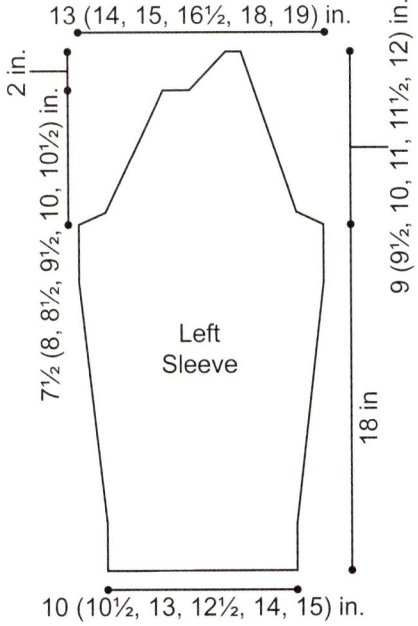

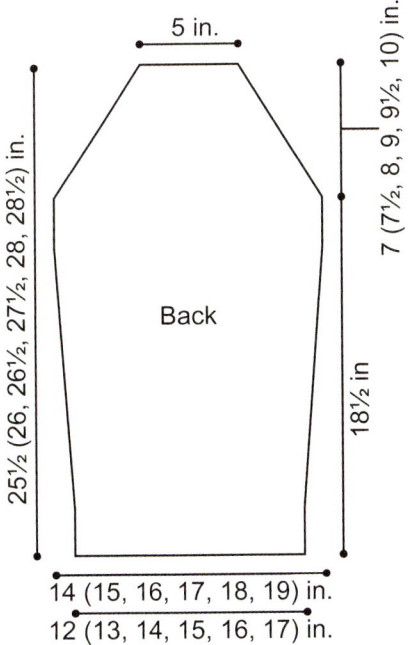

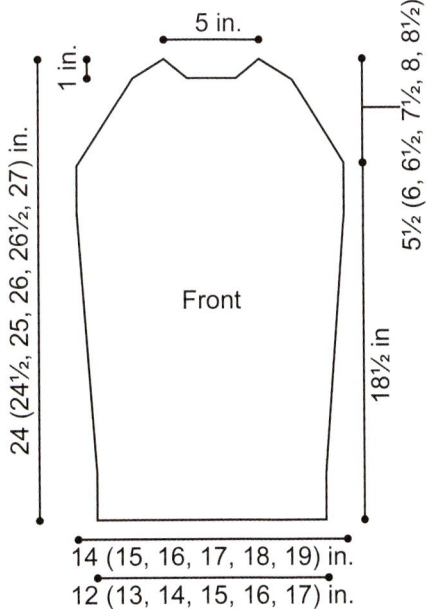

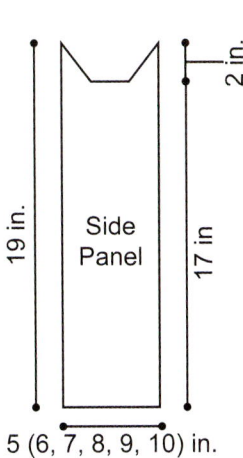

Texture Stripe Pullover

Easy

SIZES
S/M (L, 1X/2X).

MEASUREMENTS
Finished Bust About 44 (51, 57)"/112 (129.5, 145)cm
Finished Length, excluding cowl neck About 23 (24, 25)"/58.5 (61, 63.5)cm

MATERIALS
YARN
LION BRAND® Heartland®, 5.3oz/150g balls, each approx 481yd/440m (cotton/acrylic/other) (4)
- 4 (5, 6) balls in #148 Badlands (A)

LION BRAND® Homespun®, 6oz/170g balls, each approx 185yd/169m (acrylic/polyester) (5)
- 3 (4, 5) balls in #438 Garnet (B)

KNITTING NEEDLES
- One size 7 (4.5mm) circular needle, 29"/73.5cm long, *or size to obtain gauges*
- One size 9 (5.5mm) circular needle, 16"/40.5cm long

NOTIONS
- Stitch markers
- Tapestry needle

GAUGES
- 17 sts + 24 rows = about 4"/10cm in St st with smaller needles and A.
- 18 sts + 24 rows = about 4"/10cm in K1, p2 Rib with smaller needles and A.

BE SURE TO CHECK YOUR GAUGE.

PATTERN STITCHES
K1, P1 RIB WORKED IN ROWS
(worked over an odd number of sts)
Row 1 K1, *p1, k1; rep from * to end of row.
Row 2 K the knit sts and p the purl sts.
Rep Row 2 for K1, p1 Rib worked in rows.

K1, P2 RIB WORKED IN ROWS
(worked over a multiple of 3 sts)
Row 1 *K1, p2; rep from * to end of row.
Row 2 K the knit sts and p the purl sts.
Rep Row 2 for K1, p2 Rib worked in rows.

K1, P2 RIB WORKED IN RNDS
(worked over a multiple of 3 sts)
Rnd 1 *K1, p2; rep from * to end of rnd.
Rep Rnd 1 for K1, p2 Rib worked in rnds.

TEXTURE STRIPE PATTERN
Rows 1–3 With A, work in St st for 3 rows.
Rows 4 and 5 With B, knit.
Rep Rows 1–5 for Texture Stripe pattern.

NOTES
1) Pullover is worked in 4 pieces: Back, Front, and 2 Sleeves.

2) Each piece is worked back and forth in rows, beg at lower edge. Each row begins and ends with a Garter st selvedge st. Selvedge sts are used in seaming.

3) Two yarn colors are used in the Texture Stripe pattern. Do not cut yarn between color changes, just carry unused color along side of piece.

4) A long circular needle is used to accommodate the number of sts. Work back and forth on the circular needle as if working on straight needles.

Texture Stripe Pullover

5) After shoulders are seamed, sts are picked up around neck edge and cowl neck is worked in rnds on the short circular needle.

PULLOVER

BACK

With long circular needle and A, cast on 89 (104, 116) sts.

Ribbing

Row 1 (RS) With A, k1 (selvedge st), work Row 1 of K1, p2 Rib to last st, k1 (selvedge st).
Row 2 With A, k1 (selvedge st), work Row 2 of K1, p2 Rib to last st, k1 (selvedge st).
Keeping first and last st in Garter st (k every st on every row) for selvedges, continue in K1, p2 Rib until piece measures about 6"/15cm from beg, end with a WS row as the last row you work.

Main section of back

Row 1 (RS) With A, k1, work Row 1 of Texture Stripe pattern to last st, k1.
Row 2 With A, k1, work Row 2 of Texture Stripe pattern to last st, k1.
Rows 3–16 Keeping first and last st in Garter st for selvedges, continue in Texture Stripe pattern for 14 more rows, the last row you work will be a Row 1 (WS).
Inc Row 17 (RS) With A, k1, kfb, k to last 2 sts (for Row 2 of Texture Stripe pattern), kfb, k1—you will have 91 (106, 118) sts in this row.
Row 18 With A, k1, work Row 3 of Texture Stripe pattern to last st, k1.
Rows 19–32 Keeping first and last st in Garter st for selvedges, continue in Texture Stripe pattern for 14 more rows, the last row you work will be a Row 2 (WS).
Inc Row 33 (RS) With A, k1, kfb, k to last 2 sts (for Row 3 of Texture Stripe pattern), kfb, k1—93 (108, 120) sts.
Row 34 With B, k1, work Row 4 of Texture Stripe pattern to last st, k1.
Rows 35–48 Keeping first and last st in Garter st for selvedges, continue in Texture Stripe pattern for 14 more rows, the last row you work will be a Row 3 (WS).
Inc Row 49 (RS) With B, k1, kfb, k to last 2 sts (for Row 4 of Texture Stripe pattern), kfb, k1—95 (110, 122) sts.
Keeping first and last st in Garter st for selvedges, continue in Texture Stripe pattern until piece measures about 21 (22, 23)"/53.5 (56, 58.5)cm from beg, end with a WS row as the last row you work.

Shape shoulders

Row 1 (RS) Bind off 6 (7, 8) sts, work in Texture Stripe pattern as established to last st, k1—89 (103, 114) sts.
Rows 2–4 Rep Row 1 for 3 more times—71 (82, 90) sts.

Shape neck and continue to shape shoulders

Row 5 (RS) Bind off 5 (6, 7) sts, work in Texture Stripe pattern as established over next 20 (23, 26) sts (for a total of 21 (24, 27) sts on right needle) for right side of neck; join a 2nd ball of yarn and bind off 19 (22, 22) sts for back neck, work in Texture Stripe pattern as established to last st, k1 for left side of neck—you will have 21 (24, 27) sts for right side and 26 (30, 34) sts for left side.
You will now work both sides AT THE SAME TIME with separate balls of yarn.
Row 6 On left side, bind off 5 (6, 7) sts, work in Texture Stripe pattern as established to end of side; on right side, bind off 3 sts, work in Texture Stripe pattern as established to end—18 (21, 24) sts for right side and 21 (24, 27) sts for left side.
Row 7 On right side, bind off 5 (6, 7) sts, work in Texture Stripe pattern as established to end of side; on left side, bind off 3 sts, work in Texture Stripe pattern as established to end—13 (15, 17) sts for right side and 18 (21, 24) sts for left side.
Row 8 On left side, bind off 5 (6, 7) sts, work in Texture Stripe pattern as established to end of side; on right side, bind off 2 sts, work in Texture Stripe pattern as established to end—11 (13, 15) sts for right side and 13 (15, 17) sts for left side.
Row 9 On right side, bind off 5 (6, 7) sts, work in Texture Stripe pattern as established to end of side; on left side, bind off 2 sts, work in Texture Stripe pattern as established

to end—6 (7, 8) sts for right side and 11 (13, 15) sts for left side.

Row 10 On left side, bind off 5 (6, 7) sts, work in Texture Stripe pattern as established to end of side; on right side, bind off 1 st, work in Texture Stripe pattern as established to end—5 (6, 7) sts for right side and 6 (7, 8) sts for left side.

Row 11 On right side, bind off rem 5 (6, 7) sts; on left side, bind off 1 st, work in Texture Stripe pattern as established to end—5 (6, 7) sts for left side only. Bind off rem 5 (6, 7) sts of left side.

FRONT

Cast on and work same as Back to Shape Shoulders.

Shape shoulders

Row 1 (RS) Bind off 6 (7, 8) sts, work in Texture Stripe pattern as established to last st, k1—89 (103, 114) sts.
Row 2 Rep Row 1—83 (96, 106) sts.

Shape neck and continue to shape shoulders

Row 3 (RS) Bind off 6 (7, 8) sts, work in Texture Stripe pattern as established over next 27 (31, 35) sts (for a total of 28 (32, 36) sts on right needle) for left side of neck; join a 2nd ball of yarn and bind off 15 (18, 18) sts for back neck, work in Texture Stripe pattern as established to last st, k1 for right side of neck—you will have 28 (32, 36) sts for left side and 34 (39, 44) sts for right side.
You will now work both sides AT THE SAME TIME with separate balls of yarn.

Row 4 On right side, bind off 6 (7, 8) sts, work in Texture Stripe pattern as established to end of side; on left side, bind off 3 sts, work in Texture Stripe pattern as established to end—25 (29, 33) sts for left side and 28 (32, 36) sts for right side.

Row 5 On left side, bind off 5 (6, 7) sts, work in Texture Stripe pattern as established to end of side; on right side, bind off 3 sts, work in Texture Stripe pattern as established to end—20 (23, 26) sts for left side and 25 (29, 33) sts for right side.

Row 6 On right side, bind off 5 (6, 7) sts, work in Texture Stripe pattern as established to end of side; on left side, bind off 2 sts, work in Texture Stripe pattern as established to end—18 (21, 24) sts for left side and 20 (23, 26) sts for right side.

Row 7 On left side, bind off 5 (6, 7) sts, work in Texture Stripe pattern as established to end of side; on right side, bind off 2 sts, work in Texture Stripe pattern as established to end—13 (15, 17) sts for left side and 18 (21, 24) sts for right side.

Row 8 On right side, bind off 5 (6, 7) sts, work in Texture Stripe pattern as established to end of side; on left side, bind off 2 sts, work in Texture Stripe pattern as established to end—11 (13, 15) sts for left side and 13 (15, 17) sts for right side.

Row 9 On left side, bind off 5 (6, 7) sts, work in Texture Stripe pattern as established to end of side; on right side,

Texture Stripe Pullover

bind off 2 sts, work in Texture Stripe pattern as established to end—6 (7, 8) sts for left side and 11 (13, 15) sts for right side.

Row 10 On right side, bind off 5 (6, 7) sts, work in Texture Stripe pattern as established to end of side; on left side, bind off 1 st, work in Texture Stripe pattern as established to end—5 (6, 7) sts for left side and 6 (7, 8) sts for right side.

Row 11 On left side, bind off rem 5 (6, 7) sts; on right side, bind off 1 st, work in Texture Stripe pattern as established to end—5 (6, 7) sts for right side only. Bind off rem 5 (6, 7) sts of right side.

SLEEVES (MAKE 2)
With long circular needle and A, cast on 61 (63, 65) sts.
Row 1 (RS) With A, k1 (selvedge st), work Row 1 of K1, p1 Rib to last st, k1 (selvedge st).
Row 2 With A, k1 (selvedge st), continue in K1, p1 Rib to last st, k1 (selvedge st).

Lower texture stripe section
Rows 1–18 Keeping first and last st in Garter st for selvedges, beg with Row 3 of pattern, work in Texture Stripe pattern for 18 rows. The last row you work will be a Row 5 (WS).

Stockinette stitch section
Cut B.
Inc Row (RS) With A, k1, kfb, k to last 2 sts, kfb, k1—63 (65, 67) sts.
Next 13 (7, 3) Rows Keeping first and last st in Garter st for selvedges, beg with a WS (purl) row work in St st (k on RS, p on WS) for 13 (7, 3) rows.
Rep Inc Row—65 (67, 69) sts.
Rep last 14 (8, 4) rows for 2 (5, 9) more times—69 (77, 87) sts.

Keeping first and last st in Garter st for selvedges, beg with a WS (purl) row work in St st until piece measures about 13"/34.5cm from beg, end with a WS row as the last row you work.

Upper texture stripe section

Keeping first and last st in Garter st for selvedges, beg with Row 1 of pattern, work in Texture Stripes pattern until piece measures about 16½"/42cm from beg. Bind off.

FINISHING

Sew shoulder seams.

Cowl neck

From RS with short circular needle and B, pick up and k 87 (99, 99) sts evenly spaced around neck edge. Place marker for beg of rnd. Join by working the first st on the left hand needle with the working yarn from the right hand needle. Work in K1, p2 Rib worked in rnds for about 9"/23cm. Bind off.

Place markers on both sides of Back and Front, about 8 (9, 10)"/20.5 (23, 25.5)cm down from shoulder seams. Sew tops of Sleeves between markers.
Sew side and Sleeve seams.

Weave in ends. •

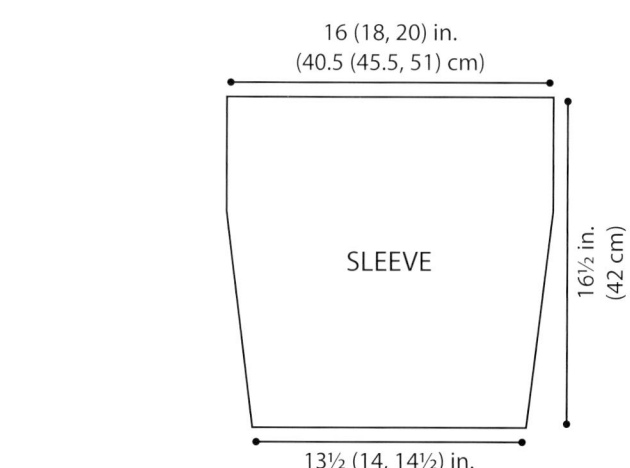

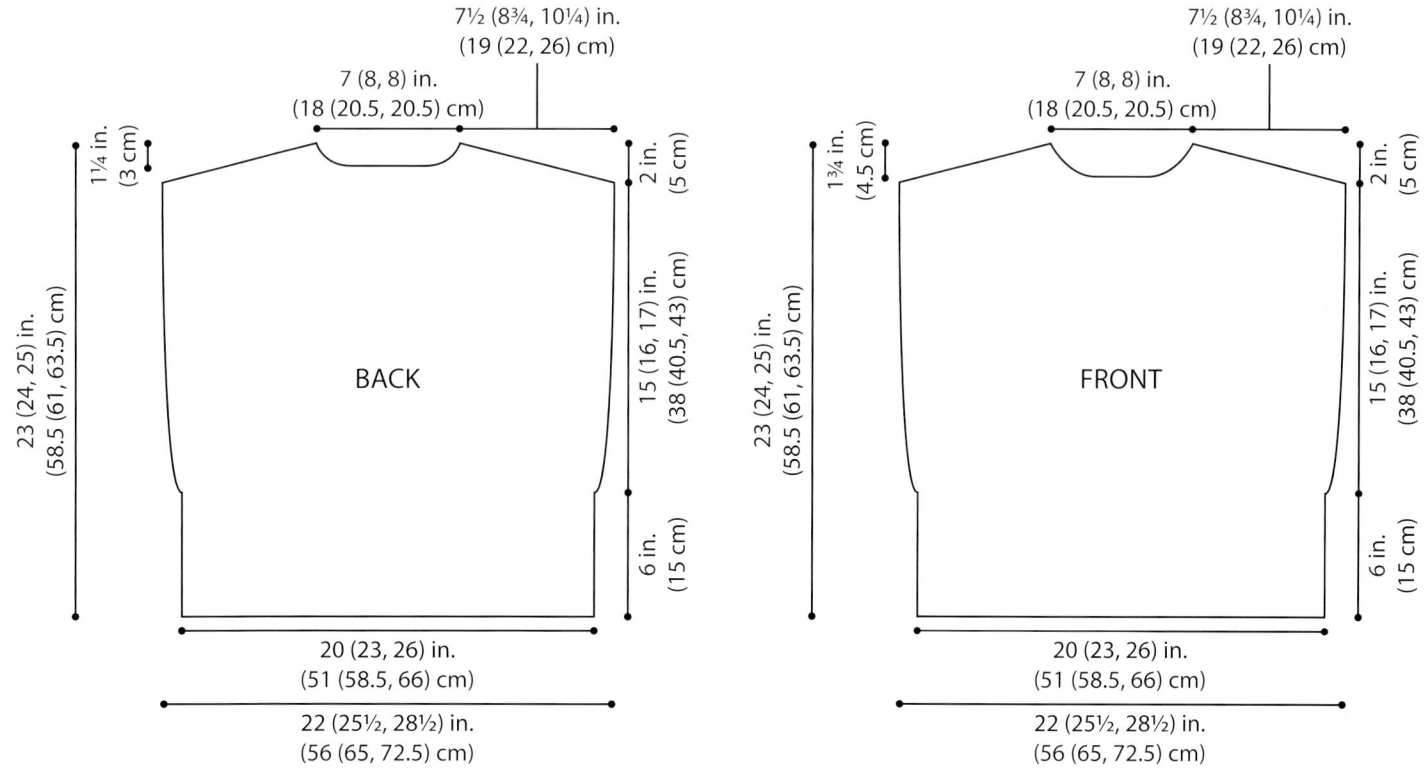

Wilhelmina Pullover

Easy

SIZES
S (M, L, 1X, 2X).

MEASUREMENTS
Finished Bust About 40 (44, 48, 52, 56)"/101.5 (112, 122, 132, 142)cm
Finished Length About 22 (22½, 23, 23½, 24½)"/56 (57, 58.5, 59.5, 62)cm

MATERIALS
YARN
LION BRAND® Comfy Cotton Blend, 7oz/200g balls, each approx 392yd/358m (cotton/polyester) (acrylic)
- 3 (4, 4, 5, 5) balls in #710 Driftwood

KNITTING NEEDLES
- One size 7 (4.5mm) circular needle, 16"/40.5cm long, *or size to obtain gauges*
- One size 7 (4.5mm) circular needle, 29"/73.5cm long
- One size 6 (4mm) circular needle, 16"/40.5cm long

NOTIONS
- Stitch markers
- Tapestry needle

GAUGES
- 18 sts + 24 rows = about 4"/10cm in St st with larger needle.
- 24 sts = about 4"/10cm in ribbing pattern of Back Rows 1 and 2.

BE SURE TO CHECK YOUR GAUGE.

NOTES
1) Pullover is made in 4 pieces: Back, Front, and 2 Sleeves.
2) Each piece begins with ribbing at lower edge and then is worked in St st.
3) A circular needle is used to accommodate the number of stitches. Work back and forth in rows on the circular needle as if working on straight needles.
4) Turtleneck is worked in the rnd on a circular needle.

PULLOVER
BACK
With longer needle, cast on 91 (99, 109, 117, 127) sts.
Row 1 (WS) P1, *k1, p1; rep from * to end of row.
Rows 2 K the knit sts and p the purl sts.
Rep Row 2 until piece measures about 2"/5cm from beg, end with a WS row as the last row you work.
Work in St st (k on RS, p on WS) until piece measures about 14"/35.5cm from beg, end with a WS row as the last row you work.

Shape armholes
Row 1 (RS) Bind off 5 (5, 7, 9, 9) sts, k to end of row—you will have 86 (94, 102, 108, 118) sts in this row.
Row 2 Bind off 5 (5, 7, 9, 9) sts, p to end of row—81 (89, 95, 99, 109) sts.
Work even in St st until armholes measure about 7 (7½, 8, 8½, 9½)"/18 (19, 20.5, 21.5, 24)cm, end with a WS row as the last row you work.

Shape Back Neck
Row 1 (RS) K24 (28, 29, 31, 34) sts for right side of neck; join a 2nd ball of yarn and bind off center 33 (33, 37, 37, 41) sts for back neck, k to end of row for left side of neck—24 (28, 29, 31, 34) sts on each side of neck.

You will now work both sides AT THE SAME TIME with separate balls of yarn.
Row 2 Purl over both sides using separate balls of yarn.

Wilhelmina Pullover

Row 3 On right side, k to last 3 sts, ssk, k1; on left side, k1, k2tog, k to end of side—23 (27, 28, 30, 33) sts on each side of neck.
Rep Rows 2 and 3 once more—22 (26, 27, 29, 32) sts on each side of neck.

Work even in St st on each side using a separate ball of yarn for each side until armholes measure about 8 (8½, 9, 9½, 10½)"/20.5 (21.5, 23, 24, 26.5)cm.
Bind off each side using separate balls of yarn.

FRONT
Cast on and work same as Back until armholes measure about 5½ (6, 6½, 7, 8)"/14 (15, 16.5, 18, 20.5)cm, end with a WS row as the last row you work.

Shape front neck
Row 1 (RS) K30 (34, 35, 37, 40) sts for left side of neck; join a 2nd ball of yarn and bind off center 21 (21, 25, 25, 29) sts for front neck, k to end of row for right side of neck—30 (34, 35, 37, 40) sts on each side of neck.
You will now work both sides AT THE SAME TIME with separate balls of yarn.
Row 2 On right side, p all sts; on left side, bind off 3 sts, p to end of side.
Row 3 On left side, k all sts; on right side, bind off 3 sts, k to end of side—27 (31, 32, 34, 37) sts on each side of neck.
Row 4 On right side, p all sts; on left side, bind off 2 sts, p to end of side.
Row 5 On left side, k all sts; on right side, bind off 2 sts, k to end of side—25 (29, 30, 32, 35) sts on each side of neck.
Row 6 Purl over both sides using separate balls of yarn.
Row 7 On left side, k to last 3 sts, ssk, k1; on right side, k1, k2tog, k to end of side—24 (28, 29, 31, 34) sts on each side of neck.
Rep Rows 6 and 7 for 2 more times—22 (26, 27, 29, 32) sts on each side of neck.

Work even in St st on each side using a separate ball of yarn for each side until armholes measure same as Back armholes.
Bind off each side using separate balls of yarn.

SLEEVES (MAKE 2)
With longer needle, cast on 50 (52, 54, 56, 58) sts.
Row 1 (WS) *K1, p1; rep from * to end of row.
Row 2 K the knit sts and p the purl sts.
Rep Row 2 until piece measures about 2"/5cm from beg, end with a WS row as the last row you work.

Work in St st until piece measures about 3"/7.5cm from beg, end with a WS row as the last row you work
Inc Row (RS) K1, M1L, k to last st, M1R, k1—52 (54, 56, 58, 60) sts.
Work even in St st for 7 (7, 7, 5, 5) rows.
Rep Inc Row—54 (56, 58, 60, 62) sts.
Rep last 8 (8, 8, 6, 6) rows 9 (9, 3, 13, 8) more times—72 (74, 64, 86, 78) sts when all inc have been completed.

Sizes S (1X) ONLY
Work even in St st until piece measures about 19½ (20½)"/49.5 (52)cm from beg.
Bind off.

Sizes M (L, 2X) ONLY
Work even in St st for 5 (5, 3) rows.
Rep Inc Row—76 (66, 80) sts.
Rep last 6 (6, 4) rows 0 (8, 7) more times—76 (82, 94) sts when all inc have been completed.
Work even in St st until piece measures about 19½ (20, 20½)"/49.5 (51, 52)cm from beg.
Bind off.

FINISHING
Sew shoulder seams.

Mock turtleneck
From RS with larger 16"/40.5cm needle and beg at either shoulder seam, pick up and k 94 (94, 102, 102, 110) sts evenly spaced around neck edge.
Place marker for beg of rnd and join by working the first st on the left hand needle with the working yarn from the right hand needle.
Purl one rnd.
Rnd 1 *K1, p1; rep from * to end of rnd.
Rep Rnd 1 until turtleneck measures about 2"/5cm.
Change to smaller 16"/40.5cm needle.
Knit 4 rnds.
Bind off loosely.

Sew in Sleeves.
Sew side and Sleeve seams, leaving 2"/5cm at lower edge of sides unsewn for slits.

Weave in ends. •

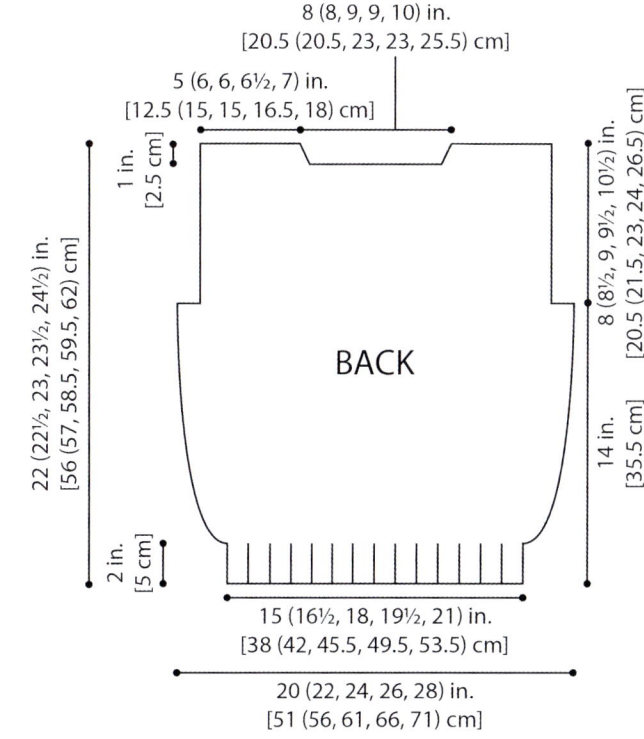

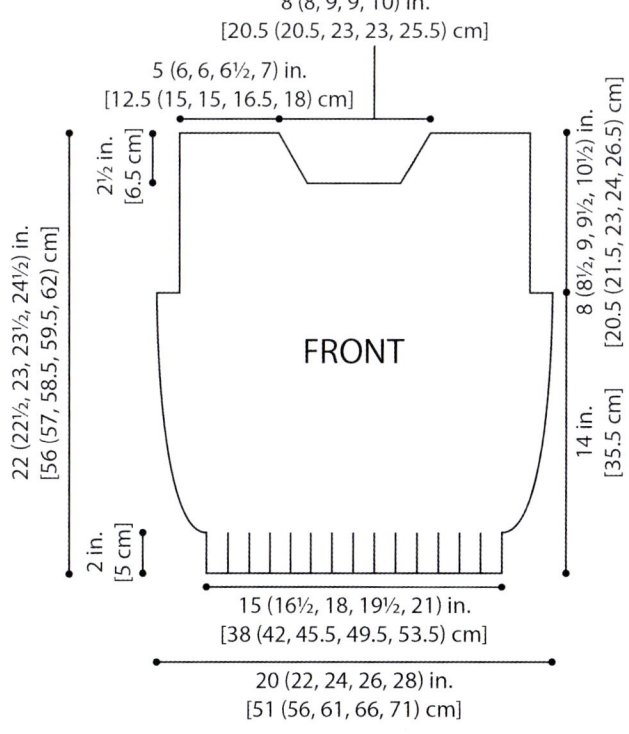

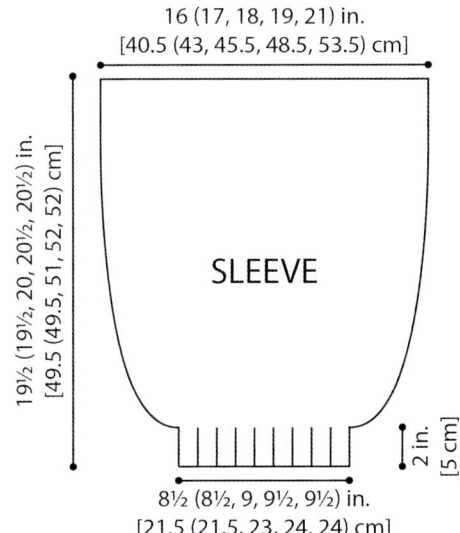

Zooey Raglan Pullover

Intermediate

SIZES
XS/S (M/L).

MEASUREMENTS
Finished Bust About 38 (45)"/96.5 (114.5)cm
Finished Length, excluding neck edging About 22 (23)"/56 (58.5)cm

MATERIALS
YARN
LION BRAND® Vanna's Choice®, 3½oz/100g balls, each approx 170yd/156m (acrylic)
- 2 (3) balls in #177 Sage (A)

LION BRAND® New Basic 175™, 3½oz/100g balls, each approx 170yd/156m (acrylic)
- 2 (3) balls each in #173 Thyme (B) and #108 Juniper (C)
- 1 (2) balls in #098 Cream (D)

KNITTING NEEDLES
- One size 9 (5.5mm) circular needle, 16"/40.5cm long, *or size to obtain gauge*
- One size 9 (5.5mm) circular needle, 36"/91.5cm long

NOTIONS
- Stitch markers
- Stitch holders
- Tapestry needle

GAUGE
16 sts + 20 rows = about 4"/10cm in Rev St st.
BE SURE TO CHECK YOUR GAUGE.

CABLE CAST ON
*Insert right needle between first 2 sts on left needle, wrap yarn and pull through (as if knitting a st), transfer new st to left needle; rep from * for desired number of sts.

STRIPE SEQUENCE
*Work 4 rows/rnds with C, 2 rows/rnds with B, 2 rows/rnds with D, 2 rows/rnds with A, and 2 rows/rnds with B; rep from * for Stripe Sequence.

NOTES
1) Pullover is worked in one piece from the top down.
2) Neck shaping is worked first, back and forth in rows, then piece is joined and worked in the round.
3) The upper body is worked to underarms, then work is divided and sleeves and lower body are worked separately to lower edge.
4) Sleeves are worked back and forth in rows. Lower body is worked in rnds.
5) The yarn color is changed following Stripe Sequence throughout. Carry colors not in use loosely up the side edge of piece.
6) When working in rows, work back and forth in rows on the circular needle as if working on straight needles.

PULLOVER
With shorter needle and C, cast on 52 (58) sts.

NECK
Shape neck
Row 1 (RS) With C, p10, pm, p to last 10 sts, pm, p10.
Row 2 Pm on left needle, then with C, cast on 3 (4) sts using Cable Cast On, k to end of row, sm as you come to them—you will have 55 (62) sts in this row.

Row 3 Pm on left needle, then with C, cast on 3 (4) sts using Cable Cast On, beg over sts just cast on, [p to 1 st before next marker, pfb, sm, pfb] 4 times, p to end of row—66 (74) sts. Change to B. Continue to sm as you come to them.
Row 4 With B, cast on 4 (5) sts using Cable Cast On, k to end of row and sm as you come to them—70 (79) sts.
Row 5 With B, cast on 4 (5) sts using Cable Cast On, p to end of row—74 (84) sts. Change to D.
Row 6 With D, cast on 5 (6) sts using Cable Cast On, [k to 1 st before next marker, kfb, sm, kfb] 4 times, k to end of row—87 (98) sts.
Row 7 (RS) With D, cast on 5 (6) sts using Cable Cast On, k to end of row—92 (104) sts.

Join to complete neck shaping
Change to A.
Row 8 (WS) With A, cast on 8 sts using Cable Cast On, without working any sts TURN and spread sts evenly along needle—100 (112) sts. Cut B, C, and D.

As you beg the next rnd, join piece into a rnd by working first st on left-hand needle with working yarn from right-hand needle. Do not place beg of rnd marker now; it will be placed in the next rnd.
Inc Rnd (RS) With A, [p to 1 st before next marker, pfb, sm, pfb] 4 times, then p to 2nd marker, this marker is now the beg of rnd marker change it to a different color—108 (120) sts.
Change to B.
Next 2 Rnds With B, p to end of rnd. Change to C.
Inc Rnd With C, [pfb, p to 1 st before next marker, pfb, sm] 4 times—116 (128) sts.
Rep last 3 rnds for 12 (14) more times, continue to change yarn color following

Zooey Raglan Pullover

Stripe Sequence, and change to longer circular needle when sts no longer fit comfortably on shorter needle—212 (240) sts when all inc have been completed.

DIVIDE FOR LOWER BODY AND SLEEVES

Continue to change yarn color following Stripe Sequence throughout.

Next Rnd K64 (74), remove marker, slip next 42 (46) sts onto a st holder for first sleeve, remove marker, cast on 12 (16) sts for underarm, k64 (74), remove marker, slip next 42 (46) sts onto a st holder for second sleeve, remove marker, cast on 6 (8) sts, pm for new beg of rnd, cast on 6 (8) sts for underarm, remove old beg of rnd marker—152 (180) sts.

LOWER BODY

Work even in Rev St st worked in rnds (p every st on every rnd) and continue changing yarn color following Stripe Sequence until piece measures about 10"/25.5cm from divide. Change to A.
Next Rnd With A, knit.
Next Rnd With A, *k1, p1; rep from * to end of rnd.
Rep last 2 rnds for about 2"/5cm.
Bind off.

SLEEVES

Continue to change yarn color following Stripe Sequence. Work back and forth in rows.
Cast-On Row 1 (WS) Cast on 7 (9) sts; from WS, k42 (46) sts of one sleeve from holder—49 (55) sts.
Cast-On Row 2 Cast on 7 (9) sts, p to end of row—56 (64) sts.
Row 3 Knit.

Dec Row (RS) P1, p2tog, p to last 3 sts, p2tog, p1—54 (62) sts.

Next 9 (7) Rows Work even in Rev St st worked in rows (p on RS, k on WS) for 9 (7) rows.

Next Row Rep Dec Row—52 (60) sts.

Rep last 10 (8) rows for 5 (6) more times—42 (48) sts. Work even in Rev St st until sleeve measures about 14"/35.5cm from cast-on rows, end with a WS row as the last row you work.

Change to A.

Next Row (RS) With A, knit.

Next Row (WS) With A, *k1, p1; rep from * to end of row.

Rep last 2 rows for about 4"/10cm.

Bind off.

Rep for 2nd sleeve.

FINISHING

Sew sleeve and underarm seams.

Neckband

From RS with shorter needle and A, pick up and k 88 (94) sts evenly spaced around neck edge. Place marker for beg of rnd and join by working first st on left-hand needle with working yarn from right-hand needle.

Rnd 1 *K1, p1; rep from * around.

Rnd 2 Knit.

Rep Rnds 1 and 2 for 4"/10cm.

Bind off.

Weave in ends. •

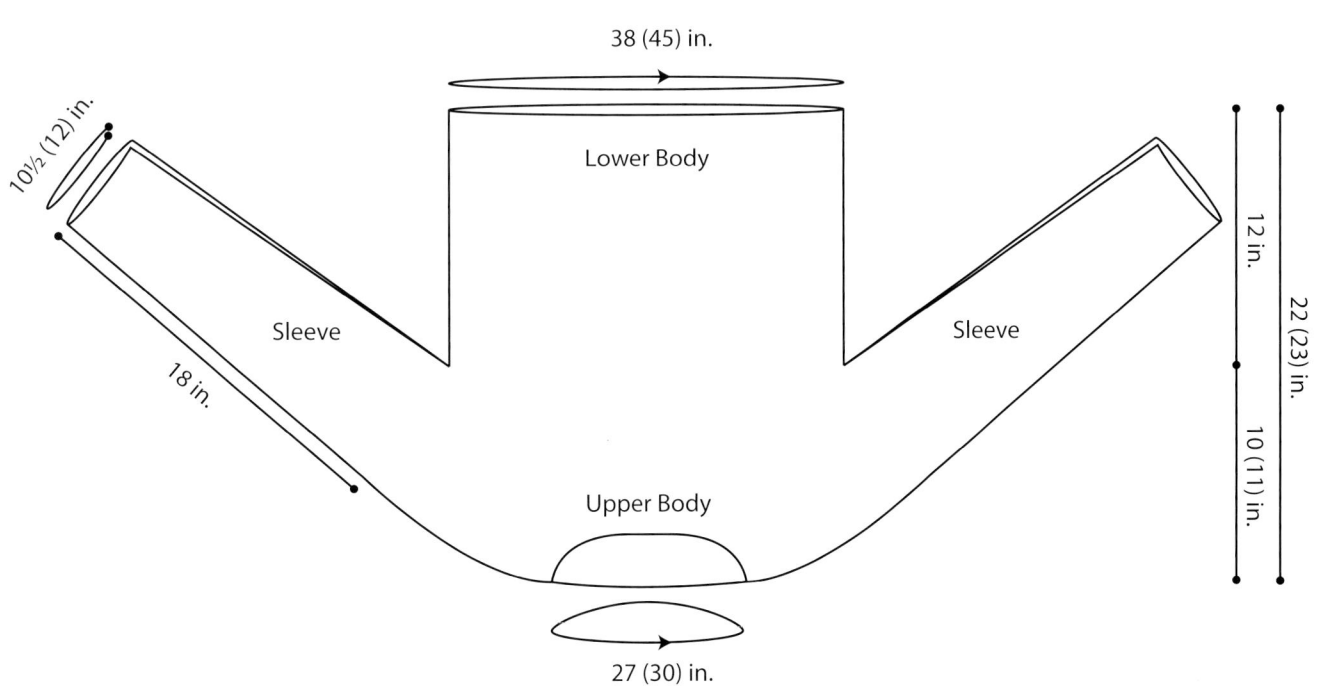

Cowl Neck Pullover

●●●
Intermediate

SIZES
S/M (L, 1X/2X).

MEASUREMENTS
Finished Bust About 48 (54, 60)"/122 (137, 152.5)cm
Finished Length (excluding cowl neck) About 24½ (25½, 26½)"/62 (65, 67.5)cm

MATERIALS
YARN
LION BRAND® Vanna's Choice®, 3½oz/100g balls, each approx 170yd/156m (acrylic)
- 5 (6, 7) balls in #110 Navy (A)
- 2 (3, 3) balls in #117 Electric Blue (B)

KNITTING NEEDLES
- One size 8 (5mm) knitting needle, 36"/91.5cm long, *or size to obtain gauge*
- One size 6 (4mm) circular needle, 16"/40.5cm long

NOTIONS
- Stitch markers
- Tapestry needle

GAUGE
12½ sts + 18½ rows = about 4"/10cm in rev St st with larger needles.
BE SURE TO CHECK YOUR GAUGE.

NOTES
1) Pullover is worked in 4 pieces: Front, Back, and 2 Sleeves.
2) Front and Back are worked side to side in rev St st.
3) Each row of all 4 pieces begins and ends with a Garter stitch selvedge stitch. Selvedge stitches create a neat edge for seaming and picking up stitches.
4) After shoulders are seamed, stitches are picked up around neck edge and cowl neck is worked in St st.
5) Stitches are picked up along lower edge of Back and Front and lower band is worked in Garter stitch.
6) Work back and forth in rows on the circular needle as if working with straight needles.

PULLOVER
FRONT
Right front
With larger needle and A, cast on 22 (24, 26) sts.
Row 1 (WS) Knit.
Row 2 Cast on 4 sts, beg over sts just cast on, k1, p to last st, k—you will have 26 (28, 30) sts in this row.
Rows 3 and 4 Rep Rows 1 and 2—30 (32, 34) sts in Row 4.
Row 5 Knit.
Row 6 Cast on 4 sts, k1, p to last st, pfb—35 (37, 39) sts.
Rows 7 and 8 Rep Rows 1 and 2—39 (41, 43) sts.
Row 9 Knit.
Row 10 Cast on 32 sts, k1, p to last st, k1—71 (73, 75) sts.
Row 11 Knit.
Row 12 K1, p to last st, pfb—72 (74, 76) sts.
Rows 13–17 K1 (selvedge st), work in rev St st (p on RS, k on WS) to last st, k1 (selvedge st).
Row 18 Rep Row 12—73 (75, 77) sts.
Rows 19–36 (42, 48) Rep Rows 13–18 for 3 (4, 5) more times—76 (79, 82) sts in last row worked.

Shape neck
Row 1 (WS) Bind off 3 sts, k to end of row—73 (76, 79) sts.
Row 2 K1, p to last st, k1.
Row 3 Bind off 2 sts, k to end of row—71 (74, 77) sts.

Cowl Neck Pullover

Rows 4 and 5 Rep Rows 2 and 3—69 (72, 75) sts in Row 5.
Row 6 K1, p to last st, k1.
Row 7 Bind off 1 st, k to end of row—68 (71, 74) sts.
Rows 8–11 Rep Rows 6 and 7 for 2 more times—66 (69, 72) sts in Row 11.
Rows 12–16 (18, 20) K1, work in rev St st to last st, k1. Change to B.
Next 8 Rows With B, k1, work in rev St st to last st, k1. Change to A. Cut B. Continue with A only.
Next 4 (6, 8) Rows K1, work in rev St st to last st, k1.
Next Row (WS) Cast on 1 st, k to end of row—67 (70, 73) sts.
Next Row K1, p to last st, k1.
Next Row Cast on 1 st, k to end of row—68 (71, 74) sts. Rep last 2 rows—69 (72, 75) sts in last row worked.
Next Row K1, p to last st, k1.
Next Row Cast on 2 sts, k to end of row—71 (74, 77) sts. Rep last 2 rows—73 (76, 79) sts in last row worked.
Next Row K1, p to last st, k1.
Next Row Cast on 3 sts, k to end of row—76 (79, 82) sts.

Left front
Row 1 (RS) K1, p to last 2 sts, p2tog—75 (78, 81) sts.
Rows 2–6 K1, work in rev St st to last st, k1.
Row 7 K1, p to last 2 sts, p2tog—74 (77, 80) sts.
Rows 8–25 (31, 37) Rep Rows 2–7 for 3 (4, 5) more times—71 (73, 75) sts in last row worked.
Next Row (WS) Knit.
Next Row Bind off 32 sts, p to last st, k1—39 (41, 43) sts.
Next Row Knit.
Next Row Bind off 4 sts, p to last st, k1—35 (37, 39) sts.
Next Row Knit.
Next Row Bind off 4 sts, p to last 2 sts, p2tog—30 (32, 34) sts.
Next Row Knit.
Next Row Bind off 4 sts, p to last st, k1—26 (28, 30) sts. Rep last 2 rows—22 (24, 26) sts in last row worked.
Next Row Knit.
Bind off.

BACK
Left back
Cast on and work same as right front to Shape Neck.

Shape neck
Row 1 (WS) Bind off 2 sts, k to end of row—74 (77, 80) sts.
Row 2 K1, p to last st, k1.
Row 3 Bind off 1 st, k to end of row—73 (76, 79) sts.
Rows 4 and 5 Rep Rows 2 and 3—72 (75, 78) sts in Row 5.
Rows 6–16 (18, 20) K1, work in rev St st to last st, k1. Change to B.
Next 8 Rows With B, k1, work in rev St st to last st, k1. Change to A. Cut B. Continue with A only.
Next 10 (12, 14) Rows K1, work in rev St st to last st, k1.
Next Row (WS) Cast on 1 st, k to end of row—73 (76, 79) sts.
Next Row K1, p to last st, k1.
Next Row Cast on 1 st, k to end of row—74 (77, 80) sts.
Next Row K1, p to last st, k1.
Next Row Cast on 2 sts, k to end of row—76 (79, 82) sts.

Right back
Work same as left front.
Bind off.

Sleeves (make 2)
With larger needle and B, cast on 28 (30, 32) sts.
Rows 1–4 Knit.
Row 5 (WS) K1 (selvedge st), k to last st, k1 (selvedge st).
Row 6 K1 (selvedge st), p to last st, k1 (selvedge st).
Rep Rows 5 and 6 until piece measures about 4"/10cm from beg, end with a WS row as the last row you work.
Inc Row (RS) K1, pfb, p to last 2 sts, pfb, k1—30 (32, 34) sts.
Next 5 (5, 3) Rows K1, work in rev St st to last st, k1.
Rep Inc Row—32 (34, 36) sts.
Rep last 6 (6, 4) rows for 7 (9, 11) more times—46 (52, 58) sts.
Rep Rows 5 and 6 until piece measures about 19 (18½, 18)"/48.5 (47, 45.5)cm from beg. Bind off.

FINISHING

Sew shoulder seams.

Cowl neck

From RS with smaller needle and A, pick up and k 68 (74, 82) sts evenly spaced around neck edge. Place marker for beg of rnd. Join by working the first st on the left hand needle with the working yarn from the right hand needle. Work in St st worked in rnds (k every st on every rnd) for about 7½"/19cm.
Next Rnd Purl.
Next Rnd Knit.
Next Rnd Purl.
Bind off.

Lower band

From RS with larger needle and A, pick up and k 70 (79, 92) sts evenly spaced along lower edge of Front.
Work in Garter st (k every st on every row) for 4 rows.
Bind off.
Rep along lower edge of Back.

Place markers on both sides of Back and Front, about 7 (8, 9)"/18 (20.5, 23)cm down from shoulder seams. Sew tops of Sleeves between markers.
Sew side and Sleeve seams.

Weave in ends. ●

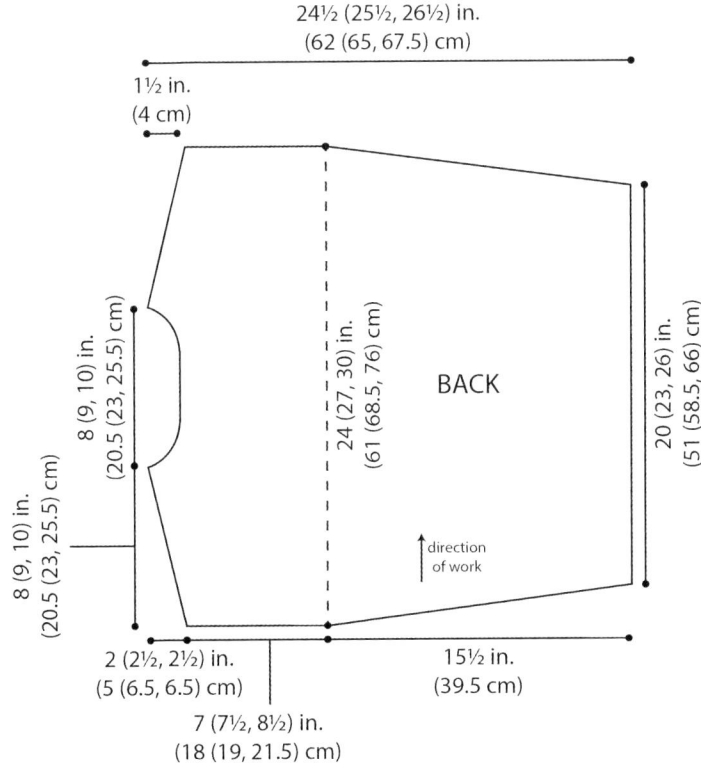

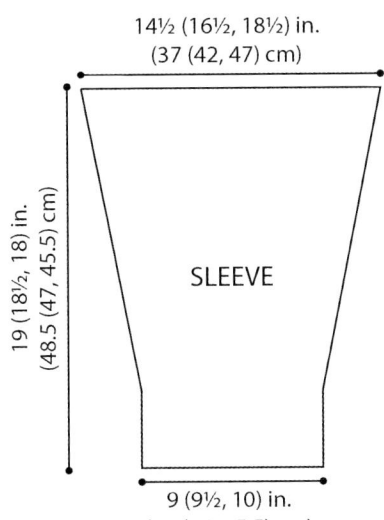

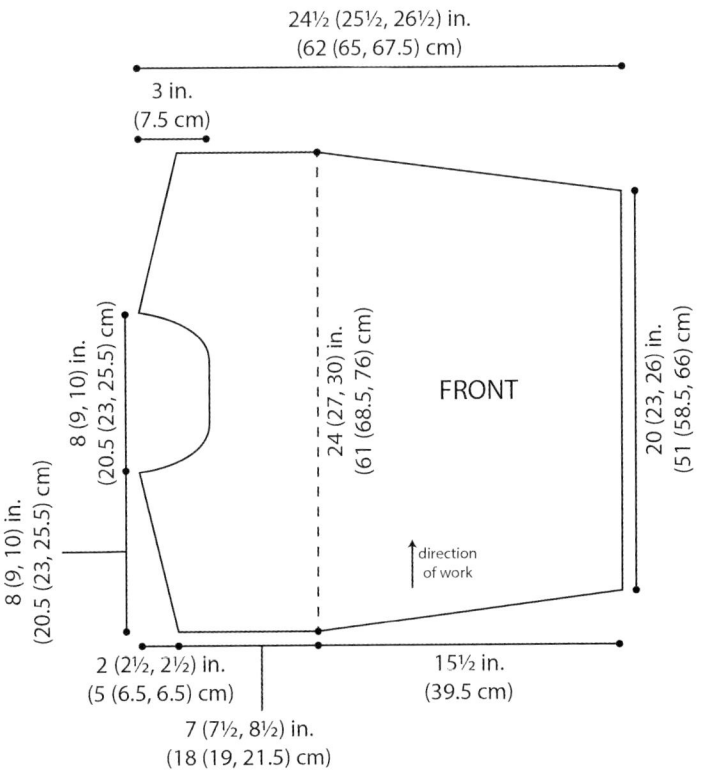

Cobble Hill Pullover

Easy

SIZES
S (M, L, 1X, 2X).

MEASUREMENTS
Finished Chest About 42 (46, 49, 52, 55)"/106.5 (117, 124.5, 132, 139.5)cm
Finished Length About 28 (28½, 29, 29½, 30)"/71 (72.5, 73.5, 75, 76)cm

MATERIALS
YARN
LION BRAND® Mandala®, 5.3oz/150g balls, each approx 590yd/540m (acrylic)
- 3 (3, 4, 4, 4) balls in #214 Centaur

KNITTING NEEDLES
- One size 6 (4mm) circular needle, 29"/73.5cm long, *or size to obtain gauge*
- One size 4 (3.5mm) circular needle, 16"/40.5cm long
- One size 4 (3.5mm) circular needle, 29"/73.5cm long

NOTIONS
- Stitch markers
- Stitch holders
- Tapestry needle

GAUGE
20 sts + 28 rows = about 4"/10cm in St st with larger needle.
BE SURE TO CHECK YOUR GAUGE.

PATTERN STITCH
K2, P2 RIB
(multiple of 4 sts + 2 additional sts)
Row 1 (WS) K2, *p2, k2; rep from * to end of row.
Row 2 K the knit sts and p the purl sts.
Rep Row 2 for K2, p2 Rib.

NOTES
1) Pullover is made in 4 pieces: Back, Front, and 2 Sleeves.
2) All pieces are worked in St st (k on RS, p on WS), beginning with ribbed lower edges.
3) The long circular needles are used to accommodate the large number of sts. Work back and forth in rows on the circular needle as if working on straight needles.
4) Neckband is worked in rounds on short circular needle.

PULLOVER
BACK
With longer and smaller needle, cast on 106 (114, 122, 130, 138) sts.
Work in K2, p2 Rib until piece measures about 2½"/6.5cm from beg, end with a WS row as the last row you work. Change to larger needle.
Beg with a RS (knit) row, work in St st (k on RS, p on WS) until piece measures about 17"/43cm from beg, end with a WS row as the last row you work.

Shape armholes
Rows 1 and 2 Bind off 6 (6, 10, 10, 14) sts, work in St st to end of row—you will have 94 (102, 102, 110, 110) sts at the end of Row 2.
Dec Row 3 (RS) K1, ssk, work in St st to last 3 sts, k2tog, k1—92 (100, 100, 108, 108) sts.
Row 4 Work in St st to end of row.
Rep Rows 3 and 4 three more times—86 (94, 94, 102, 102) sts.

Cobble Hill Pullover

Work even in St st until armholes measure about 9 (9½, 10, 10½, 11)"/23 (24, 25.5, 26.5, 28)cm, end with a WS row as the last row you work.

Shape neck
Row 1 (RS) K27 (30 30, 33, 33) sts, place next 32 (34, 34, 36, 36) sts on a holder for neck; join a 2nd ball of yarn and k to end of row—27 (30, 30, 33, 33) sts on each side of neck.

You will now be working both sides of neck AT THE SAME TIME using separate balls of yarn.

Row 2 On first side, p to end of side; on 2nd side, p to end of side.

Row 3 On first side, k to last 3 sts of side, k2tog, k1; on 2nd side, k1, ssk, k to end of side—26 (29, 29, 32, 32) sts on each side.

Rep Rows 2 and 3 twice more—24 (27, 27, 30, 30) sts rem on each side.

Shape shoulders
Row 1 (WS) On first side, bind off 8 (9, 9, 10, 10) sts, work in St st to end of side; on 2nd side, work in St st to end of side—16 (18, 18, 20, 20) sts on first side and 24 (27, 27, 30, 30) sts on 2nd side.

Rows 2–4 Rep Row 1 for 3 more times—8 (9, 9, 10, 10) sts rem on each side at end of Row 4.

Row 5 On first side, bind off all rem sts; on 2nd side, p to end of side.

Bind off all rem sts of rem side.

FRONT
Work same as Back until armholes measure about 7 (7½, 8, 8½, 9)"/18 (19, 20.5, 21.5, 23)cm, end with a WS row as the last row you work.

Shape neck
Row 1 (RS) K32 (35, 35, 38, 38) sts, place next 22 (24, 24, 26, 26) sts on a holder for neck; join a 2nd ball of yarn and k to end of row—32 (35, 35, 38, 38) sts on each side of neck.

You will now be working both sides of neck AT THE SAME TIME using separate balls of yarn.

Rows 2 and 3 On first side, work in St st to end of side; on 2nd side, bind off 3 sts, work in St st to end of side—29 (32, 32, 35, 35) sts rem on each side at end of Row 3.

Rows 4 and 5 On first side, work in St st to end of side; on 2nd side, bind off 2 sts, work in St st to end of side—27 (30, 30, 33, 33) sts rem on each side at the end of Row 5.

Rows 6 and 7 On first side, work in St st to end of side; on 2nd side, bind off 1 st, work in St st to end of side—26 (29, 29, 32, 32) sts rem on each side at end of Row 7.

Rep Rows 6 and 7 twice more—24 (27, 27, 30, 30) sts rem on each side.

Work even in St st until armholes measure same as Back to Shape Shoulders, end with a WS row as the last row you work.

Shape shoulders
Row 1 (RS) On first side, bind off 8 (9, 9, 10, 10) sts, work in St st to end of side; on 2nd side, work in St st to end of side—16 (18, 18, 20, 20) sts on first side and 24 (27, 27, 30, 30) sts on 2nd side.

Rows 2–4 Rep Row 1 for 3 times—8 (9, 9, 10, 10) sts on each side at end of Row 4.

Row 5 On first side, bind off all rem sts; on 2nd side, k to end of side.

Bind off all rem sts of rem side.

SLEEVES (MAKE 2)
With either length smaller needle, cast on 46 (46, 50, 50, 54) sts.

Work in K2, p2 Rib until piece measures about 2½"/6.5cm from beg, end with a WS row as the last row you work.

Change to larger needle.

Beg with a RS (knit) row, work in St st for 4 rows.

Inc Row (RS) K1, M1, work in St st to last st, M1, k1—48 (48, 52, 52, 56) sts.

Work in St st for 3 rows.

Rep Inc Row—50 (50, 54, 54, 58) sts.

Rep last 4 rows 6 (7, 7, 8, 8) more times—62 (64, 68, 70, 74) sts.

Work in St st for 5 rows.

Rep Inc Row—64 (66, 70, 72, 76) sts.

Rep last 6 rows 8 (8, 7, 8, 7) more times—80 (82, 82, 84, 88, 90) sts when all inc have been completed.

Work even in St st until piece measures about 17 (17, 18, 18, 18)"/43 (43, 45.5, 45.5, 45.5)cm from beg, end with a WS row as the last row you work.

Shape cap

Next 2 Rows Bind off 2 (2, 3, 3, 4) sts, work in St st to end of row—76 (78, 78, 82, 82) sts rem.

Dec Row 1 (RS) K1, ssk, work in St st to last 3 sts, k2tog, k1—74 (76, 76, 80, 80) sts.

Next Row Work in St st to end of row.

Rep last 2 rows 15 (15, 19, 20, 24) more times—44 (46, 38, 40, 32) sts rem.

Rep Dec Row 1—42 (44, 36, 38, 30) sts.

Dec Row 2 (WS) P1, p2tog, work in St st to last 3 sts, p2tog through back loops, p1—40 (42, 34, 36, 28) sts.

Rep Dec Rows 1 and 2 for 7 (7, 5, 5, 3) more times—12 (14, 14, 16, 16) sts rem.

Rep Dec Row 1 for 0 (1, 0, 1, 0) time(s)—12 (12, 14, 14, 16) sts rem.

Bind off.

Cobble Hill Pullover

FINISHING
Sew shoulder seams.

Neckband
From RS with shorter smaller needle, beg at right shoulder seam, pick up and k 8 sts evenly spaced along right back neck edge, k32 (34, 34, 36, 36) back neck sts from holder, pick up and k8 sts evenly spaced along left back neck edge to left shoulder seam, pick up and k 17 sts evenly spaced along left front neck edge, k22 (24, 24, 26, 26) front neck sts from holder, pick up and k 17 sts evenly spaced along right front neck edge—104 (108, 108, 112, 112) sts.

Place marker for beg of rnd. Join by working the first st on the left hand needle with the working yarn from the right hand needle.

Rnd 1 *K2, p2; rep from * to end of rnd.
Rep Rnd 1 for 1½"/4cm.
Bind off loosely.

Sew in Sleeves. Sew side and Sleeve seams.

Weave in ends. •

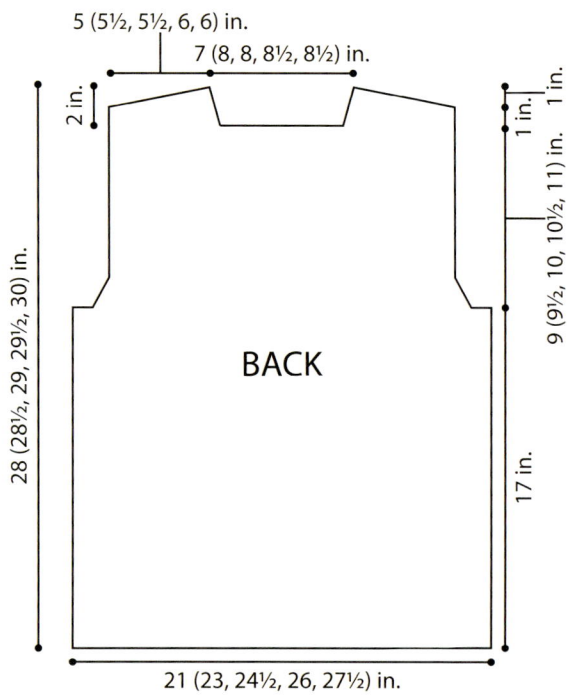

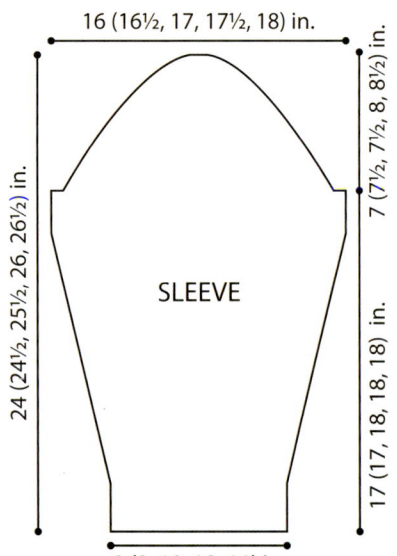

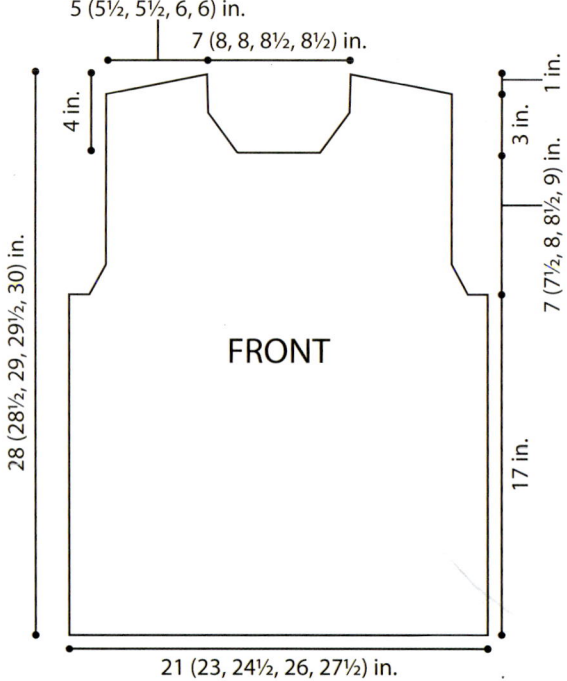